Lingam Worship

A Sacred Sexuality Guidebook for the New Earth

COPYRIGHT © JEN MCCARTY 2024

All rights reserved. No part of this publication may be reproduced, distributed, or transmitted in any form or by any means, including photocopying, recording, or other electronic or mechanical methods, without the prior written permission of the publisher, except in the case of brief quotations embodied in critical reviews and certain other non-commercial uses permitted by copyright law.

For permission requests, contact the author

Jen McCarty –

cosmicgypsy33@gmail.com

Book Front Page Cover Artist: Jen McCarty

Edition 04/06/2024

ISBN: 979-832-790-4835

DISCLAIMER NOTICE

Although the author has made every effort to ensure that the information in this book was correct at time of press, the author does not assume and hereby disclaims any liability to any party for any loss, damage, or disruption caused by errors or omissions, whether such errors or omissions result from negligence, accident, or any other cause.

This book is not intended as a substitute for the medical advice of physicians. The reader should regularly consult a physician in matters relating to his/her health and particularly with respect to any symptoms that may require diagnosis or medical attention.

I dedicate this book

to the divine masculine soul consciousness

MESSAGE FROM JEN

All of the information that I share has been received directly through my own access to the Akashic Records. Nothing that I share is regurgitated information; it is all based on downloads that I have personally received. It is so important that as you are reading these words, you exercise your own discernment and only take on as truth that which resonates for you as truth. If something does not feel true to you, then that is correct; so please do honour that.

I have been guided to speak about subject matters such as Tantra, Kundalini Energy, Twin Flames, Hieros Gamos, the Zero Point Field, and Fifth Dimensional Consciousness many times in many different ways throughout this book. The reason for the repetition of these subject matters is to act as an antidote to the heavy third-dimensional programming that has sought to indoctrinate everyone into the false belief that they are simply limited to the third dimension. This book is a reprogramming agenda of the highest order, and the way that it is delivered to you is encoded with specific intentions.

This book is published by

TABLE OF CONTENTS

BOOK TESTIMONIES x
INTRODUCTION 1
CHAPTER 1
What is the Lingam?..9
CHAPTER 2
Divine masculine came forth first 12
CHAPTER 3
Facing our sexual trauma in order to move forward 21
CHAPTER 4
What is sacred sexuality 27
CHAPTER 5
What has this all got to do with Shiva? 33
CHAPTER 6
Shadow work, sexuality, and healing our sexual trauma .37
CHAPTER 7
Inner child healing and healing our sexual trauma 45
CHAPTER 8
Pornography...51
CHAPTER 9
White Tantra..57
CHAPTER 10
Holy sexualism..63
CHAPTER 11
Healing our perception / Our sight to recognize the
holiness of our sexuality. 66
CHAPTER 12

How do we worship the Lingam?..71

CHAPTER 13

How to implement Lingam worship into your current relationship..74

CHAPTER 14

How to start a new relationship which includes Lingam worship. 81

CHAPTER 15

Why do we worship the Lingam?..84

CHAPTER 16

Working with the violet flame...88

CHAPTER 17

What happens in our life when we worship the Lingam? 91

CHAPTER 18

Lingam, worship and sacred relationships.........................95

CHAPTER 19

Women are the leaders in Tantra 100

CHAPTER 20

How the divine feminine is deeply encoded in her spiritual blueprint to worship the Lingam 106

CHAPTER 21

Twin flames and soul contracts. 109

CHAPTER 22

The spiritual impacts of loose sexuality, polyamory, polygamy, and more 112

CHAPTER 23

Intimacy avoidance and co-dependency, and how this relates to the old paradigm of relationships......................115

CHAPTER 24

How do you know if you are with your highest spiritual partner? 120

CHAPTER 25
Ascension and Lingam worship...125

CHAPTER 26
The dark side of the phallus...133

CHAPTER 27
Conclusion – Boundaries and Practices on how to work with the teachings of this book. 138

AFTERWORD..147

APPENDIX..155

BIBLIOGRAPHY 179

BOOK TESTIMONIES

The book "Honouring the Lingam" is a clarion call to the awakened human collective to restore the original template of sacredness in our relationship with each other and particularly in sexuality.

This sacred text came from the depths of the heart of an enlightened Indian sage and Shiva devotee who incarnated from the mists of time in the shape of Jen McCarty.

Her profound and intuitive insights and stark revelations shake the foundation of the old and outdated three dimensional matrix. They greatly assist the ongoing Earth Ascension by facilitating the twin flame unions, which were torn apart during the fall of Atlantis.

With fearlessness and clarity Jen McCarty blazes a trail of sacredness in the western mind – conditioned by old cliches as well as vane and animalistic traits in the sexual relationships.

This book resonates with the new and subtle Ascension energies pouring down on Earth from the galactic centre, which we as an awakened collective are duty bound to anchor and embody for the greater good of all.

~ Chad

Dear Jen,

Your books are always like beautiful pieces of music. This one in particular feels like we are taken up to the highest realms to the frequency of the angels. It truly was angelic music for the soul.

Your truthful description of the Lingam brought back so much remembrance of a time when we were fully conscious and living in peace and harmony. It resonated so deeply with my soul that this is the way it should be.

May we all release the programming that has been imposed on us about how we see the lingam and may we come back into the essence and power of who we truly are. Your words bought this all back into my consciousness of how it should be and what I have known deep down all along.
Another masterpiece by the amazing Jen!
I cannot wait to read the book!

~ Marie

In this fascinating book Jen McCarty dives deep into her spiritual awakening in Northern India many years ago and her incredible experiences in a recent return to India, to the Tamul Mountains of Arunachala the spiritual home of Lord Shiva.

In Hindu and yogic philosophy Shiva is the warrior energy and the transmuter of darkness, embodying divine masculine energy as Shanti embodies the divine feminine energy. What makes the book so absorbing is Jen's description of her direct connection with Lord Shiva and the wisdom and enlightenment he imparts to her, not only regarding our origins as twin flame masculine and feminine pairs, but also the sacred energy held in the Lingam, the phallus and the societal damage inflicted upon us by our non-remembrance of our sacred sexuality.

Jen provides guidance for journalling and guided meditation to heal sexual trauma and her deepest prayer is for humanity to embrace remembrance of our true selves as fractoids of God's energy and recognise our sexuality as an integral part of our true divine essence.

~ Claire Rodgers

Review for "Honouring the Lingam.

I am so deeply grateful to have had the privilege of reading this new masterpiece of Jens.

It's taken me two weeks to write this review after experiencing a deeply emotional transformational purge and shift. I actually felt like I was learning for the first time what the shiva Lingam is and the powerful role of the divine masculine, and this brought up so much grief within me.

Once this grief had passed a deeper remembrance has

risen within me.

This book is so powerful and activating and has completely shifted my whole perspective of every divine masculine.

I can't wait to have the physical book in my hands.

Jen you really are a portal of divine wisdom and your dedication to serve and share your knowledge is a true blessing and gift.

I highly recommend this book to everyone.

~ BS Jones

Beyond ideas of wrongdoing and right doing, there is a field.
I will meet you there.'

RUMI

INTRODUCTION

I have just returned from India. I was strongly guided to go to Arunachala in Tamul Nadu to connect with my Shiva roots. When I was 21 years old, I came to India for the first time. Upon my arrival to this sacred holy land, I travelled high up in the northern hills of the Himalayas. On reaching Chamba in Northern India an area north of Dharamsala, a group of friends and I were invited to go and stay in an orchard that belonged to our friend Junko Chowfla.

As we were all preparing to leave for the trek, a very small Italian woman ignored every group member and came up to me and said, "You must chant the mantra Om Namah Shivaya." I had never heard of the mantra Om Namah Shivaya, and to be honest, I didn't really know much about Shiva at that time, but she asked me about 50 times, and she made me promise her that I would keep repeating the mantra Om Namah Shivaya. And I so said yes.

Upon my promise to fulfil her request, we all departed Chamba and began our trek high up in the Himalayan mountains. My experience was extremely arduous as I was carrying a 25-kilo rucksack, and it was a vertical trek which lasted over 12 hours.

This was extremely challenging for my body, yet I kept chanting the mantra Om Namah Shivaya. As night fell, we reached the top of the mountain. upon our arrival, my friends went and sat and had a cup of tea by the fire, but I had a strong urge to be by myself, so I walked towards the edge of the mountaintop.

When I arrived at the top of the cliff, I looked up at the sky, and in my heart I was chanting Om Namah Shivaya. And as I looked at the sky, I saw and felt a profound flash in my third eye.

This experience showed me that prior to this moment, my third eye was sealed shut. But at that moment, in that instant, it opened, and I saw God EVERYWHERE and in everything – in every moment, in every breath, in every grain of sand, in every leaf, in every blade of grass, in every molecule of oxygen, in every drop of the ocean. My eyes could just see God everywhere.

As I met this God light, the energy moved through my body very blissfully, and when it arrived at my stomach area, I felt this enormous interfacing of this godly light with all of the fear and beliefs and Egoic identification that I had been carrying my whole entire life.

I felt the light travel underneath this pain, and I started crying tears of great, great relief because I knew in that instant that only love was real. Only love is eternal, and if it isn't love, it isn't eternal.

It was an extremely blissful and life-changing experience. And from that moment, I was never ever the same again. It lasted approximately 10 minutes,

After this experience, I was guided to go and share this with my soul brother. And that night, he and I slept under the stars like two innocent children, absolutely reborn in spiritual bliss and ecstasy.

The next morning, I woke up, and I had a direct experience of the angelic realm singing glorious remembrances of divine, eternal truth into my ears/ heart and consciousness.

This was a constant process which activated extraordinarily blissful surges of energy into my spine. The rushes started at the base of my spine, and they ascended all the way up to my crown and out again. As these blissful thoughts of truth and knowing and remembrance poured forth from the spiritual realms, I experienced an absolute bombardment of what I soon found out later were kundalini rushes

I was experiencing a Kundalini initiation, expansion and awakening.

On that particular day, I experienced a profound revelation regarding my identity and purpose within this lifetime. It became evident to me that my principal objective whilst incarnated in this beautiful vessel was to hold and maintain the child-like genius flame that burned eternally within myself and validate that for all children that came into my energetic sphere be they big children or small children.

Somehow, this deep truth was being downloaded and transmitted into my consciousness, and with it, a deep penetrating understanding that my mission in life is to validate the sacred – validate the childlike - validate the authentic genius flame that resides within all of us prior to the bombardment of fear programming that seems inevitable for each soul that incarnates into this third-dimensional Matrix….

I was also shown that I would be transmitting this spiritual energy and remembrance through music, and I was also told that I would be a fashion designer, which I went on to be for 11 years before I started sharing my spiritual teachings.

This experience lasted six months, and it was a continuous, perpetual bombardment of Kundalini rushes and blissful sacred remembrances about the true nature of reality, about the nature of God, consciousness. I understood deeply and implicitly what the word eternity means, what the word forever means, what the word timeless means, what the word infinity means. And I was bathing in the deepest, deepest knowing and remembrance of what love truly truly is in the universal sense.

A big part of my experience on the mountain was connected to meeting my soul brother, Christopher. As I looked into his eyes, I saw such exquisite beauty and the hand of God in such a perfect way that I recognized him as Christ. And in the moment of my recognition that he was the holy one, the beloved son of God, I realized that he was reflecting my personification as the Christ.

He reflected the truth of who I am as a feminine Christed being. And in the moment of that realization, it was like a billion light bulbs went off as I realized that every single one of my brothers and sisters is a Christed being, I implicitly remembered and understood that when we are born, we all possess that seed/ blueprint, and we all have the potential to actualize our Christed self in our lifetime.

This was all such an extraordinary revelation to me, and I would never have believed any book or teacher if they had told me this. It was something that I had to experience myself directly. The absolute knowing and remembrance of the holiness of every minute aspect of creation, large and small.

My experience on the top of the mountain brought me into a vibration of spiritual ecstasy. I was ecstatically surrendering my ego to my higher self. I was open and grounded in every conceivable moment of that experience. I was fully earthed, and I attribute this greatly to my astrological placements and a very heavy emphasis on the energies of Capricorn.

This ecstatic spiritual experience lasted in its acute phase for six months. When I arrived back in England in January 1996, I encountered the next stage of my awakening experience; Upon landing back in the UK

I was still holding the absolute knowing and knowledge of my true God self and everyone else's true God self.

However, the nature of the experience underwent a significant shift, and the subsequent phase ushered me into an extraordinary journey. The illuminating light I had initially encountered in India transitioned beyond the honeymoon phase, signalling the time for me to confront and transmute both my personal shadow aspects and the shadow remnants and threads rooted in my ancestry.

This phase posed challenges to my physical well-being, yet it was simultaneously marked by profound bliss and enlightenment. Engaging with my shadow self and ancestral shadows became a vital and enlightening process whilst also offering a profoundly crucial service to humanity. Embracing the newfound role of a spiritual warrior, I fearlessly delved into every aspect of the shadow self, bringing forth the light of the God-self and fostering a remembrance of the holy presence, which with every encounter I met, faced and ultimately alchemized back into Love.

I was engaged in a psychospiritual process which saw me confronting issues of abandonment and rejection, betrayal by self and others, and all manner of difficult emotional patterns. All of this had to be experienced in order to be able to be moved through, and ultimately out, of my physical vessel.

This phase of my awakening lasted for quite a few years.

One of the extraordinary gifts from my awakening in India was psychic powers. After my awakening, whoever I met in the form of a brother or sister, as I looked at them, my soul blueprint consciousness registered and fully remembered who they are.

As their vibrational frequency connected with my divine consciousness, I accessed their Akashic records, allowing me to instantly comprehend details about their soul gifts, patterns, and wounds. I could perceive their soul journey across past, present, and future perspectives. While I didn't consistently disclose everything I perceived, I made it a point to share relevant insights when fitting. This ability to recognize and understand each individual as a reflection of myself or a brother or sister in Christ has definitely been one of the most pertinent and prolific gifts that have come out of my Awakening on top of the Himalayan mountain...

On the mountaintop, I found my parents, Mother Father God. And I realised that every single one of God's children is my brother and sister. We are all one blood-spiritual family. Therefore, whenever I meet one of my family members, I rejoice because we are all one; I recognise you. I recognise your vibratory signature, and our souls meet in the place of the one living Heart of our eternal creator, God.

So, this, in a nutshell, is my spiritual awakening

experience, which has to be the preface for this offering that I bring forth after my return from Arunacharla, the seat of the Sidhars, the Rishi, the Literal abode of Lord Shiva.

My initiation into the spiritual tradition of Southern India has been the greatest, most intense fuel to my spiritual fire that I have ever experienced. And from this place, I bring forth this holy, sacred, divine remembrance that was shown to me at the foot of the abode of Lord Shiva – Arunachala Mountain, whereby there are eight Lingam shrines that circumvent the Holy Mountain. Indeed, Shiva is a representation of the Lingam. And in my time in Arunachala, I was graced with a divine meeting and encounter with Lord Shiva himself.

This profound meeting brought with it an initiation into working with and deeply inner-standing the holy Lingam, and in the pages to come, we will embark on a very sacred and extraordinary remembrance of the sexual polarity codes that are yours and that are mine, remembrances that have been stored safely in the tantric temples of beloved India. Remembrances of who we are as embodiments and as fractals of God source energy.

What an exciting journey we are all on.

CHAPTER 1

WHAT IS THE LINGAM?

Before we proceed further, I feel it is important to share a generic definition of what a Lingam is so that everyone has a basic introduction and understanding going forward.

The Shiva Linga, or lingam, serves as a symbolic representation of Lord Shiva in Hinduism, and temples dedicated to this powerful deity often feature a Shiva Linga. This sacred emblem encapsulates the energies of the world and beyond.

The Shiva Linga stands as a silent symbol of Lord Shiva, representing the formless, omnipotent being.

In addition to its role in Hindu tradition, various metaphysical disciplines have embraced the Shiva Linga. In this context, it refers to a specific stone from an Indian river believed to possess healing powers for the mind, body, and soul.

To comprehend the dual uses of the term "Shiva Linga," it's essential to delve into each aspect separately, beginning with its origin. Despite their apparent differences, both interpretations are interconnected, sharing an underlying meaning linked to Lord Shiva.

From my personal perspective

The Shiva lingam symbolizes the yoni, representing the divine feminine aspect of creation and the Lingam/phallus embodies the masculine aspect of creation.

This emblem signifies the union of spirit and matter and holds profound power when we engage, connect, and commence working with this symbol of extraordinary potency.

This book is principally devoted to awakening the wisdom that recognizes the deep value of devotion to the divine masculine and his sacred symbol, the Shiva lingam.

The Shiva Lingam is a symbol of power, and if you have not worked with a Shiva lingam, then this is a specific invitation to you to gift yourself with a Lingam ASAP in order to harness the most transformation from this sacred text.

As a rising humanity and the divine feminine, we have emerged to embody a profound remembrance. This remembrance is intended to facilitate healing from ancestral traumas related to sexuality and violation. Using potent spiritual tools and practices, we aim to unravel egoic identifications by immersing ourselves in the transformative fire of our holy, eternal God self.

This book is devoted to igniting the flame of deep sacred remembrance, particularly within the divine feminine and all those resonating with the divine feminine polarity energy. Whether you embody the feminine polarity energy as a female, or carry the male polarity energy, this is the essence we address.

This book is coming from a place of speaking from an energetic perspective with regard to the Yoni's eternal promise to be deeply devotional towards the phallus, which will be referred to in this book as the Lingam.

CHAPTER 2

DIVINE MASCULINE CAME FORTH FIRST

When I arrived in Arunachala, I met a wonderful elderly Indian man working opposite Ramanas Ashram in Tiruvanemeli; upon meeting this incredible divine masculine who had devoted his life to worshipping Lord Shiva, I knew I was going to buy a Shiva Lingam from him, and I knew it would happen at the right moment.

A few days passed after our encounter, and being in close proximity to Shiva's authentic vibrational resting place, Holy Mount Arunachala, I came to the realization that I belong to the Shiva lineage.

This understanding dawned upon me through my spiritual awakening, which was initiated by chanting the mantra Om Namah Shivaya. This sacred mantra has directly linked me to Shiva, making me a soul intricately connected to the Shiva lineage.

Therefore, it was a very big deal for me to go to Arunachala. When I arrived, being so close to the mountain, I experienced an extraordinarily powerful meeting with the energy of Lord Shiva, and truly, words literally cannot describe what happened to me.

When I arrived in Arunachala. I felt like an energy came into my being and completely took over every part of my bodily functional experience. I was flawed.

All of my habits and routines were completely absconded as this enormous ignition of the Shiva flame burned ceaselessly within me. I encountered the omnipresent aspect of our Lord Shiva and experienced an overwhelming sense of perfection. His outer being intensely enveloped me, and simultaneously, I realised that I am an embodiment of that divine essence. This profound realisation and remembrance left me in bed, barely able to function.

I had to find a way to navigate and embrace the wave of meeting and becoming Shiva, which had led to fully activating the flame of Shiva within my own being.

Each day, my meditations were getting more intense and powerful. My third eye was burning. I was having visions that were beyond anything I had ever known. There was a crystalline alignment with the absolute knowing of my destiny. Situations that I was destined to experience in the future – I was actually experiencing them in that moment..

All of these expansion experiences led me to extend my beloved practice of yoga as all I could do was allow my body to stretch and find comfort in this fire that I had found myself in the centre of.

And so, I did yoga, and I breathed, and I rested, and I looked after myself.

I met a peacock who landed in front of me in a small alley that I lived in, who I now know was the Sidhar Sadguru Sri Brahma who appears to his initiates as a peacock.

Many, many, many things happened in that time in the Tamul Mountains of Arunachala.

One day, I was meditating, and I had been contemplating very deeply about creation and about how this physical creation, rocks and water, air and people and animals experience how it all came into being. I very, very deeply wanted to have those questions answered. That was the general theme of my consciousness during my time on the mountain. This brought me to the question of the origin of the twin souls Adam and Eve and how they arrived on this earthly plane from the spiritual realms…

The veil between the spiritual and physical realms is very thin in places such as Arunachala, and I experienced that whenever I asked deep questions, the answers came very quickly and often from very unusual sources.

At this time, when I was contemplating deeply about the origin of Adam and Eve, I was spontaneously guided to watch my favourite children's program from when I was younger, which is called "Monkey Magic." Miraculously, the opening theme tune to this wonderful program was sent to me whilst I was in India.

The theme tune to this show tells a story that when the world was originally created, there were four land masses in a square shape. And through the alchemy of sun, water and moon, those land masses all merged together, and life was born .

So, In this web of desiring to fully understand the creation story, I sought to know and remember about the divine feminine and the divine masculine and how they, as divine twins, were born.

By this point, I had aligned with my own personal Lingam hand made by the elderly Indian devotee from the rocks of Arunachala mountain itself...

As I held the Lingam in my hand, I fell to my knees at the moment I truly realized who Lord Shiva is and that he is a symbolic representation of the Divine masculine energy who, like a warrior bursts forth from the spiritual planes.

I was shown that the masculine jumps first from the spiritual realms into the realm of matter and illusion and duality and separation, and God gave him the Lingam – his phallus as a rope, energetically designed to keep him eternally connected to the spiritual realms.

I was shown that as he held that rope / Lingam, he would always remember he was safe. He would always remember his connection to God: That feeling of holding his Lingam would be his lifetime link with his God self.

These visions made me weep with compassion when I saw that the Divine masculine was holding on for dear life to his Lingam.

I knelt in awe as the revelation unfolded before me – within divine pairs like Shiva and Shakti, Magdalene and Yeshua, and Radha and Krishna, and all eternal twin flame pairs, there was a united decision to transition from the spiritual realms to the physical realms.

As these revelations poured through, I felt the deepest love and compassion for the masculine soul: for the bravery it took to come out of the spiritual realms into this dense realm of matter and illusion.

And that was when I was shown that the divine masculine soul consciousness took the hit as the frontline way-showers ushering in the physicalisation of spirit into matter.

As their divine masculine souls came forth, they took the hit to experience the most acute, primal remembrances of pain and separation. As I held the hand-carved shiva Lingam, I instantly felt this great vulnerability from the divine masculine and simultaneously the great bravery of the divine masculine soul.

It's important to say at this point that this is not a universal truth. This is my experience. If this doesn't resonate for you, this is absolutely perfect because what I am sharing is my personal direct experience, and I'm sharing my story to hopefully trigger memories deep within your soul of the promise that you made to worship the divine.

I was shown that the divine masculine stood on the front line energetically to receive the harsh experiences of war, pain, separation, blood brutality, aggression, all of the most extraordinarily challenging experiences for the God self. The masculine had taken on the role of experiencing that.

Growing up in a feminist and socialist home, I very much rejected the notion of masculine leadership. And I always deeply questioned why the Bible spoke of Adam being born first and Eve being created out of the rib of Adam.

This made no sense to me, but in my time in the Holy mountain of Arunachala, the penny finally dropped as I was shown that the spiritual world belongs to the feminine and the physical world really belongs to the masculine energy.

And therefore, when we collectively made the descent from the spiritual realms into the physical realms, knowing that we are all created as a divine pair (as depicted in the Genesis story, all Hindu mythology, including the tarot and all Christian Norse, Egyptian and Incan mythology). Over and over again, we see the journey of the twin souls descending from the spiritual realms and being born into the physical realms.

With this newfound understanding and connection as to what the Shiva Lingam actually is – a rope that the masculine was given in order to hold onto during moments of great fear and terror at the illusionary experience of separation from God source energy, He was also given the great gift of every time he held his sacred phallus he would always feel the comfort of God source energy eternally holding him

All of these insights were pouring through, and it became lucidly clear to me that this is indeed what actually occurred as the twin souls sat at the feet of mother, father God in preparation for their descent from the spiritual realms into the physical realm.

So therefore, with this newfound knowledge, I was receiving visions of the twin flame pair sitting at the feet of mother father God, making the decision to descend from the spiritual realms into the lower dense realms of matter.

And I was shown that in each twin flame dissension paradigm, it is the divine masculine soul who births first, i.e. individuates first from Source energy energetically.

In this individuation process, I was shown that the divine masculine is curated and designed with more square, linear edges that are connected to his warrior energy that he brings with him. This warrior energy has been created to bear the brunt of the harshest aspects of physical separation from source energy, aspects of war, murder, rape, domination, and violation.

The divine masculine absorbed All of these energies, much like a sponge, creating a safety net for the divine feminine soul to jump out of the spiritual realms into third-dimensional matter.

As the feminine aspect of the divine pair, she would not have to face the depth of challenges that these separation codes induced, as her divine masculine would handle the brunt of the burden.

I suddenly felt that all of the searching, seeking, and dot connecting I had experienced in my life culminated and I was presented with an extraordinary sense of profound clarity and understanding.

This left me with a feeling of deep love and compassion towards the divine masculine for taking on the harsh elements of the separation programming and trailblazing the path from spirit to matter.

This completely transformed my relationship with the phallus as I understood deeply and implicitly that the phallus member is such a pertinent aspect of the divine masculine consciousness and is symbolic of his masculine soul. And because of all of the pain and challenges that the masculine soul has taken on, he's absolutely worthy to receive tender love and devotion from the divine feminine who has been coded to bring pleasure, nurturance, healing, protection, and deep unfathomable love to the divine masculine and his holy sexual member.

It is this revelation which changed my life, changed my energetic frequency, and inspired me to bring forth this sacred offering.

Let us now move into the next chapter.

CHAPTER 3

FACING OUR SEXUAL TRAUMA IN ORDER TO MOVE FORWARD

We as a society have experienced much painful programming and painful experiences with regard to our sexuality.

There has been a huge culture of rape, abuse, violation, child sex abuse, and abuse towards men and women, boys and girls. If you have not experienced sexual abuse in your lifetime, most likely, it exists somewhere within your ancestral lineage. Maybe even your parents or your grandparents experienced this abuse. This abuse by the Lingam has caused an unfathomable detriment to the fabric of society and has created it such that many women are afraid of the Lingam, fearful of its power, fearful of its drive, afraid of its insatiability, afraid of its desire to dominate and abuse.

This is a huge area that has affected all of our lives in some way. Therefore, it would not be credible to move forward with this sacred text without bringing some light towards this subject.

I myself have not experienced sexual abuse in this lifetime, but I come from a family where this was an extremely prevalent thing. This made it such that I grew up with a huge fear of men, a huge fear of male sexuality. As a woman, how can we experience the softness, expansion, and suppleness of our yoni if we are meeting the lingam with such deep fear?

As we progress in our spiritual evolution and transcend the programming that has been inflicted upon us from all the different areas of our society, we encounter our own healing journey. Eventually, this brings us all to working with our sexuality and healing and recalibrating our sexuality back to its original divine template.

If you are reading these words as a feminine polarity being, I would invite you now to write out in your journal your relationship with the Lingam. Write out any fears that you have held in the past, and present, and really go deep into bringing forth a stream of consciousness, expressing many different remnants of your relationship with the Lingam – focusing particularly on programming and fear around the Lingam.

When you have done this exercise, this will offer a massive eye-opener to you and will show you areas in your own consciousness where the shadow aspects have not been interfaced with the light.

It's very important that we upgrade, heal, and transform our relationship with the Lingam so that we understand the base point whereby we are starting from.

We all have a starting point. If you are afraid of the Lingam or have a disingenuous appreciation of the Lingam because you think you should, then now would be the time to get honest with yourself.

We can only bring in the transformation codes when we are honest and face our true beliefs.

This book aims to introduce ideas and concepts that will recalibrate your relationship with the Lingam entirely. And if you are a man reading this book, it is my deepest prayer that the messages in these pages will trigger your own remembrance of your own divinity and the true role of your sacred phallus member.

It's my deepest prayer that reading these words will bring you all great comfort and excitement with regard to going forward and birthing the new age, the new dawn of sacred sexuality.

We have all grown up in a society where we have been programmed to deny our intuition, disregard our inner voices, and move forward in sexual practices and actions which we are not comfortable with.

Every time you have been penetrated when you weren't ready to be penetrated, every time you have been touched without giving your permission, all of these experiences create glitches within your sexual, energetic system – kinks in your sexual meridians, which if left unchecked, will lead to a shutting down ultimately of your libido. Therefore, going forward, it is very important that we implicitly understand the societal context in which we are currently working with.

In the West, we have been born into a society that absolutely disregards sacred sexuality. We have all been programmed to be very loose sexually to share our saliva – to share our sacred sexual juices with any Tom, Dick or Harry.

Did you know that saliva contains an energetic map of all the people that you have been intimate with? Some of these people could have had demonic entities, parasites or all manner of low vibrational beings attached to their auric field, and when they kiss you, this is automatically transferred, and unless there is some form of spiritual purification and cleansing, these demonic parasites stay living in our energetic field forever.

The sexual patterns that we have all grown up with in the West are very much a part of Kali Yuga, the Hindu name for the current time frame that we have been living in and is rapidly ending, also known as the old Earth, the old Secular world.

As we move into the new earth paradigm, it is my deep belief that we will return back to saving ourselves sexually for our true divine partner.

We will work with teachers and practices that will enable us to enhance our orgasmic potential and sexual potential, but ultimately, we will save our sacred sexual juices for our partner whom we marry and ultimately ascend with.

We are in that transitionary phase at the moment we are moving from the old world, programming around sexuality, to the new earth programming around sexuality, and this book stands in the very centre of these two worlds.

In order for us to really embody the deepest understanding of and devotion towards the Lingam, we must face our fears and traumas that may have been experienced due to the Lingam.

This is for men. We must address our programmed relationship with the Lingam, which has told us that it's okay to watch porn. It's okay to be sexually loose. It's okay to sleep with many people. This is not a way to maintain optimum sexual hygiene. This is a way to activate a diminishing of one's vital sexual life force energy, which is also connected to the raising or diminishing of one's Christ oil.

The Christ oil is released as a psychospiritual seed in the sacrum plexus every month when the Moon goes into our sun sign. Each month, a seed is released in the sacrum plexus, which if we embody right action, will ascend up into the claustrum to the midpoint of the brain, whereby a sacred serum, an oil, will be released monthly.

This oil can only be released if we are not

promiscuous and if we honour our sacred sexuality. The more we squander our vital life force energy, the more we dry up this powerful oil that holds the potential to be released every month.

I may devote a whole entire chapter to speaking about the Christ oil, but it bears mentioning here that low vibrational sexual conduct absolutely leads to the drying up and diminishing of the sacred Christ oil in the claustrum.

Please see the resources at the back of this book. I share a very powerful meditation that teaches you to raise the Christ oil from the sacrum plexus up into the claustrum

In order for us to move forward and grow as a human family, we must let go of all of these programs and practices which have sought to deeply diminish our sexual power and ultimately cause damage to us on a physical, emotional, psychological, and spiritual level. Later on in the book, we will cover these subjects in greater depth this is simply an introduction to working with the energy of healing, our relationship with the Lingam.

CHAPTER 4

WHAT IS SACRED SEXUALITY

In this chapter, I would like to talk about sacred sexuality. What is sacred sexuality? What is non-sacred sexuality? Let's start with non-sacred sexuality.

If you have read my book, Twin Flames and the event, I am sure you will remember the chapter on Atlantis whereby I share in depth what I was shown with regard to the nefarious interference that was allowed to take place by the Nephilim giants at the time of Atlantis, which ultimately proceeded to its downfall.

In my book, "Twin Flames and the Event," I share how, at the time of Atlantis, humanity was living in a fifth-dimensional consciousness, crystalline state. We were all in sacred union with our twin flames, and we lived in a culture that ultimately prepared us for that divine union.

Certainly, it was this victorious alliance that maintained the crystalline equilibrium at the heart of the magnetic North Pole, as referenced in the Bible concerning the era preceding the great flood. During the Atlantean period, there was a subversion by malevolent entities who assumed the responsibility of tampering with human DNA.

Christiline humanities DNA at that time was operating from a 12-strand, 144-codon DNA patterning, which saw all human DNA in a perfect diamond formation.

However, the nefarious Atlantean overlords used forth dimensional dark technology to interfere with the Christic blueprint of the children of God. And what proceeded was a shakeup of the diamond patterning, a scrambling of the diamond patterning, which saw to it that 10 strands of the DNA were deemed junk. And two strands of the DNA were left to cover the vital survival aspects of survival.

A huge part of the nefarious Atlantean agenda was to create cataclysmic separation between the divine pairs. These old overlords knew perfectly well that it was the divine unions which were keeping the crystalline core of the magnetic north pole in a state of blissful equilibrium. And therefore, this nefarious energy entered into the matrix and brought with it the concept of ownership, control, and war.

This manifested as the overlords trying and successfully persuading many of the divine masculine's to leave their divine feminines in order to participate in their overlords wars over ownership of land mass. And this cataclysmic separation between the divine twin flames activated what can only be termed a soul tear, resulting in many divine feminines perpetually incarnating with a core wound of abandonment and many divine masculines perpetually incarnating with a wound of guilt and avoidance.

At this time, it is very essential that I offer this perspective, which I received from my spiritual team with regards to speaking from my perspective on the subject matter of sacred sexuality. So, it is my deepest understanding that at the time of Atlantis we lived in a society whereby when a child or divine being was born, it was understood that they were going to be paired with their highest sexual partner, their divine other, their twin soul. There were many tantric temples that were created in order to prepare the souls for this eventual sexual merge with their divine counterpart.

The Atlantean knowledge and truth held it such that remembrance of the power and potency of the truly polarized masculine and feminine force was at the forefront of the structure of the culture and society, and therefore it was deemed the most important aspects of one's incarnation that this holy relationship happen and flourish.

So, there would've been very little, if any, sexual connection with any other person other than your divine counterpart. And it was a wholly monogamous society, with marriage being deemed the highest honour within your lifetime.

Sacred sexuality in these modern days has got a very, very long way to go. And there may be people who read this book who do not agree with my beliefs and opinions on sacred sexuality, and it's very important that we all know that that's okay.

This book holds the conclusions that I have come to on my spiritual journey. And if they resonate with you, that is beautiful. And if they don't, that is also beautiful.

So, what I have been shown with regards to sacred sexuality is that we must awaken from this very dark nefarious programming which sought to entrain a belief that it is okay for us to have multiple sexual partners in our lifetime.

It's time to really question now whether that is true. In my humble opinion I believe that we must, as a society, place our sexuality and sexual encounters in the holiest department of our divine consciousness.

It is absolutely imperative that we understand the spiritual and energetic implications of sexual connections with people that we don't know, don't want to be and have absolutely no intention of having a relationship with.

We must awaken to the remembrance that our saliva contains an energetic blueprint of all of the lovers /sexual partners that we have been with. And every time we kiss someone, we pass on those energetic patterns to each person that we sexually engage with.

It is my deepest prayer that those of you reading these words will join this holy sexual revolution where we preserve ourselves for our one true beloved, where we restore our faith that this beloved is within us and without us.

Please read my book "Twin Flames and the Event." This will help you restore your faith. And it is my deepest prayer that your heart resonates with these sacred words and that you share this message with everyone in your life who you really, really love.

Sacred sexuality is understanding that we are all gods and goddesses we embody the potential of Yeshua and Magdalene, Shiva and Parvati, and Krishna and Rhadarani.

These aspects are Gods within the omnisphere, but they are also aspects of our own eternal nature as there is only one self, and that self has the power and ability to fragment into billions and billions of aspects and millions of personalities.

We all hold that core Godliness in our Christed blueprint Self.

Non-sacred sexuality is a result of the programming that we have all received, programming which has made us believe that it's okay to be loose sexually, and that its okay to watch pornography and have multiple sexual partners.

Non-sacred sexuality is having sex with someone, connecting intimately with someone, whom you do not love.

Non-sacred sexuality is speaking in a dishonouring way about your sexuality or someone else's.

Non-sacred sexuality is the strongest attack that has been sent forth to beautiful humanity. And this is the time that we start pulling out those bullets because those bullets do not belong to us.

We are fractals and fragments of God source energy. We are holy to our core and our sexuality is the holiest aspect of our nature.

Sacred sexuality is the understanding that lovemaking must happen by the altar, and In the temple. Lovemaking must be recognised as the holy act that it truly is – the act of God and Goddess herself coming together ultimately with the potential to birth brand new life and give an opportunity to a brand new soul to experience this expression of physicality.

I hope from these words, you now have a much more solid sense of sacred sexuality and non-sacred sexuality.

CHAPTER 5

WHAT HAS THIS ALL GOT TO DO WITH SHIVA?

In this chapter, I would like to talk about my personal relationship with Shiva and the revelations that have been born of this deep connection.

As I mentioned in the opening chapters, my experience in Arunachala was exactly what I needed to reignite the powerful spiritual flame that burns ceaselessly within me and all of us.

My soul guided me absolutely to the perfect place, considering I was a Shivite due to my third eye blasting open and the subsequent Kundalini awakening that preceded it through chanting the mantra Om namah shivaya.

My relationship to the mantra Om namah shivaya is deeply connected to my personal connection and love affair with Lord Shiva. When I received my Shiva Lingam from Arunachala which was calved, from the stone from Arunachala Mountain, I went home and did a very, very deep yoga practice and meditation. When I was meditating, I was guided to pick up the Shiva Lingam and connect with it.

I had never connected with a Shiva Lingam before, so in many ways this was an initiation experience for me. As I held the Lingam, I experienced an intense blast of Shiva's energy, which somehow entered primarily through my third eye chakra, my heart chakra, my solar plexus chakra and my base chakra.

I experienced a bolt of Shiva's energy earthing and grounding in my being. And in that moment, I felt like my consciousness merged with Shiva.

From that place, I perceived consciousness with Shiva's eyes, and I was shown that Shiva represents love, wisdom, and courage regarding the deepest aspects of duality consciousness.

I was shown that Lord Shiva is the aspect of the Godhead who comes forth as the warrior archetype. He spews forth from the high spiritual realms, and this warrior spirit is so brave and relentlessly wise.

I was shown that it is the energy of Shiva that primarily meets and interfaces with the rawist aspect of consciousness. The energy of Lord Shiva can be found in the deepest darkness of matter.

I was being repeatedly shown over and over again that Shiva's aspect births first from the spiritual realms as the warrior spirit who has incarnated to be the transmuter of all darkness in the physical realm.

Shiva's warrior energy is deeply symbolic of the masculine warrior archetype who is brave enough to step out of the blissful spiritual realms into dangerous and unchartered waters within the realm of matter.

I was shown that Shiva's Trident is a symbol of his warrior nature and that he has come forth with this warrior energy to meet head-on and ultimately transmute all darkness.

I was shown that as Lord Shiva jumps from the spiritual realms into the physical realms, he's given the phallus as a symbol of a rope, which, when he holds it, will connect him with his God source energy.

I fell to my knees in recognition of the bravery and courage vulnerability and beauty of the divine masculine. And I realised that archetypally, a huge aspect of the role of the divine feminine is to be the nurturer, the soother, the one who brings great pleasure and comfort to the warrior aspect, which is the divine masculine, which was brave enough to descend from the spiritual realms into the physical realms.

Lord Shiva showed me many, many deep, un-communicable things that day. As I became one with the Shiva Lingam, I realised at that moment that energetically there is only one Godself.

God is the mighty ocean, and we are all droplets of that ocean. But yet, as droplets, we hold the identical patterning of God source energy.

As I connected with Lord Shiva, I realized I was tapping into the archetype residing within myself. At that moment, I transformed into the Yin Yang symbol, with my awareness standing at the symbol's centre, embracing my identification with the Shiva warrior aspect. Simultaneously, I grasped, at the profound and incomprehensible level of my being, that I am also the beloved of Shiva. In my role as the divine feminine, my purpose is to nurture, soothe, and provide love and protection to my divine masculine, particularly to his core identity embodied in the phallus member, symbolizing his masculine polarity soul.

Overwhelmed by this realization, I knelt down once more, recalling the codes and frequencies of Lord Krishna. I reflected on the deep, eternal devotion that Radharani holds for her divine consort Krishna. This led me to observe similar divine partner archetypes in major religions and mythologies, recognizing a common thread of sexuality, romance, divine partnership, and expression in the sacred union of masculine and feminine energies. All the dots were coming together finally I was overwhelmed with remembrance.

CHAPTER 6

SHADOW WORK, SEXUALITY, AND HEALING OUR SEXUAL TRAUMA

As I mentioned previously, when I was in Arunachala , the energies were very intense and I was left bedridden a lot of the time. On one occasion when I ventured out, I had a very dark experience with a massage therapist in India. The interesting thing is that I dreamt about this experience, which actually was a minor sexual violation….

The experience I had with this Indian masseuse brought me to a place of deep shame, regret and a feeling of judgment towards myself that I had not exerted boundaries that would protect me from such an experience.

Whilst swimming in the ocean of complex feelings of shame, disappointment and disgust, it was only through entering this emotional depth that Lord Shiva could come and meet me.

As I sat in the discomfort of this experience, knowing that it was a minor discomfort compared to the profound violation that has afflicted many souls on earth for eons, I held onto the deep feeling of embodied darkness. It was in that lowest moment that Lord Shiva presented himself to me, appearing like a flash of overwhelming knowing, reassuring me that he was with me in this vibrational place.

Only by journeying to this dark place was I able to resonate with and embody the vibration of Lord Shiva.

I saw his form in front of me with my inner eye and was overwhelmed with emotion at the love he was exuding towards me. I began to receive the most extraordinary transmission. And it felt like his third eye was sending streams of information into my third eye about the divine masculine and about who the divine masculine is. He was transmitting to me that Shiva is symbolic of the divine masculine energy, and Shakti is the Symbol of the divine feminine energy.

As I encountered Shiva's energy, he revealed to me his Trident, symbolizing the spiritual battle he wages on the front line of consciousness. As these symbols permeated my awareness, I implicitly grasped that in the spiritual realms, where all polarized energies fully merge into the essence of the divine mother, the divine feminine energy, it is in the moment when Spirit individuates and descends into matter. It is the divine masculine that initiates that initial spark, and the reason for this is because the physical world reflects outer masculine energy, while the spiritual world mirrors the inner feminine realm.

It all clicked into place. The Genesis story of Adam being the first to emerge suddenly made perfect sense. I fully grasped that it was the divine masculine energy that burst forth initially from the spiritual realms. In that moment of birth, he had to confront head-on the energies of separation, pain, blood, fear, competition, and battle, along with the energy of God's love – eternally accompanying his arrival from the spiritual planes to the physical plane.

Part of his divine purpose was to take the hit, take the brunt of the separation experiment in order to protect the feminine and ensure that when she makes her descent from the spiritual realms into the physical realm, into her polarized feminine form, she will be endowed with the vibrations of nurturance, unconditional love, and a softness which simply was not what the masculine soul consciousness had contracted to experience.

In the moment of this revelation, which literally was happening in flashes, I fell to my knees in devotion and gratitude towards the divine masculine, for my eyes had opened to who the divine masculine truly is. I wept with compassion for his suffering and bravery and my soul sang a song of deep love and adoration towards the divine masculine consciousness.

Shiva came forth, and he showed me the symbol of the Lingam and how his Lingam is the rope that extends energetically back to God consciousness, and when he holds the Lingam, that is when he feels at one with his God self. When he puts his hands firmly around his Lingam, always in that moment, he feels one with his God self.

I was shown that the Lingam is a spiritual gift from the universe given to bring great comfort to the divine masculine soul. Shiva then showed me that the Lingam, the phallus, is worthy of recognition for what it truly is: the true symbol of the divine masculine force.

I was shown that it is absolutely appropriate to approach the Phallus with profound and everlasting reverence and recognition of what the Phallus truly is: The Phallus is God. The phallus is the rope that leads back to God, and it is a gift for the masculine and it is a gift for the feminine – indeed it is a great gift for all of creation.

As we awaken to this deep spiritual knowing and ecstatic tantric remembrance, we heal all thought forms, timelines, ancestral knots, and karmic corruptions pertaining to sexual abuse and violation, not only for ourselves individually, but also for the entire collective consciousness.

The energy of devotion, worship, and recognition of what the Phallus truly represents holds such a high frequency that it resonates as an extraordinary note within the symphonic registrar of the highest realms.

In its vibrational presence, all lower tones and entrenched patterns begin to dissolve instantly.

We have all experienced trauma. We have all experienced violation because ultimately there is only one self that has fragmented into billions and billions of individualized aspects. And whether we have experienced the violation in this lifetime or a previous lifetime, or whether we have perpetuated it in this lifetime or a previous lifetime, we have all experienced everything.

Sexual violation, misconduct and deep, dark, damaging programming have got to be recognized and called out now in order for us to leave behind this atrocious cesspit of confusion that has been enforced upon asleep humanity.

As awakened humanity, we are now empowered to choose our own programming regarding our sexuality. We are awakening to the realization that if we don't take control and ownership of our consciousness, there are countless external forces seeking to influence us. These forces have operated through the fourth-dimensional moon matrix reincarnation loop, ensnaring nearly every soul except for the self-realized avatar souls, who remain unaffected by this dark program matrix.

These avatar souls and highly evolved souls are intelligent enough to question the enforced narrative from an early age, which enables them to step out of the hijacked programming agenda, of which 99% of humanity has been sadly a victim.

Healing our sexual trauma is deeply connected to inner child work. I have been very, very blessed to heal my own inner trauma through the development of a healing modality that I devised entitled Quantum Time Travel Therapy (QTTT). I was blessed to receive information about a meditation technique which guided me to travel back in time as my present self to meet my younger little girl self –to parent her, and to bring her the healing and encouragement that she had been waiting for.

Through this time travel healing modality, I experienced the unravelling of all of the knots of trauma that were locked into my energetic system. And so, I would highly recommend finding a healing modality that works for you, that will enable you to heal and parent your inner child. In fact, I will devote an entire chapter in this book to speaking about inner child healing.

The story that I have shared in this chapter is the reason why you hold this book in your hand, and I will never in all my days forget the impact of that meeting with Lord Shiva and the information that I received.

It's important to know that this teaching will be echoed throughout all the pages of this book as this truly is the essence of the new sexuality awakening codes.

The gift for the divine masculine in reading these words is finally being seen, finally being understood, finally being recognized as the Holy Son of God that he truly is.

The gift for the divine feminine is letting go of extremely dark programming that has had her acting out in inauthentic ways with regards to her sexual conduct, enabling her to regroup and align with the truth codes around sacred sexuality and the path of white tantra, which we shall discuss in further chapters.

How can this information serve you?

This information has come forth to water seeds of knowing that you hold within your own consciousness as a divine feminine, that your divine masculine has had to face very different and specific challenges to you, and your divine masculine is holding that warrior archetype energy.

It would be my deepest prayer that reading these words will bring a layer of profound spiritual compassion and recognition towards your divine masculine understanding, his fragility, understanding his resilience, understanding his bare-faced courage to come back into this world as a man and face and embody all of the trauma that the masculine has had to experience as part of this experiment in duality.

It would be my deepest hope and prayer that you approach your divine masculine in a holy way. And if you are a man reading these words, in that case, it is my deepest prayer that you align with a far deeper understanding, connected to a stream of eternal wisdom that is held in these words and the pattern of these words – may you awaken and remember who you are as God's son, as a fractal of God source energy in a masculine body owning a holy Lingam, a sacred phallus.

It would be my sincere prayer that you purify your relationship with your phallus and understand that there has been an agenda which has sought deeply and profoundly to degrade the phallus and indeed all aspects of your sacred sexuality.

And it is my deepest prayer that you get a handle on this programming and expose it as the lie that it truly is, that you may align with the eternal. knowing that you are always connected to God source energy and your phallus is a symbol of your bravery and power. It is worthy of being cherished, adored, and devoted to.

There is so much for us to discuss. Let us move on now to the next chapter.

CHAPTER 7

INNER CHILD HEALING AND HEALING OUR SEXUAL TRAUMA

To carry on from the last chapter, I would like to speak about inner child healing and, indeed, all aspects of healing our sexual trauma.

One of the most fundamentally important truths I have remembered on my spiritual awakening path is that no one is coming here to save me. My consciousness is creating this reality, and as Neville Godard says, "Everyone is me popped out." I understand that it all comes down to me, and I have fully awakened to the knowing and remembrance that the outer is a reflection of my inner subconscious and conscious configuration patterns.

Therefore, if something is harming me from an external perspective, I must adjust my perception on the inner realms of consciousness in order to experience a shift and transformation with this issue on the external plane.

With this newfound understanding and recollection, I delved deep within myself and unearthed the voice of my higher self. I could distinguish it clearly because, in my spiritual awakening, I had come to realize that only love is real. Through this awakening,

I learned to differentiate between the voice of the Egoic fear consciousness and the voice of my true, eternal, loving higher self. I had diligently trained myself to adhere solely to the guidance of the loving, kind, and wise aspect of my consciousness.

I trained myself to pay no attention to my consciousness's negative, fearful aspect. Commitment to this was a game changer for me.

When I committed to this decision, this was the first fundamental step I took in healing all of my trauma.

All that we have to contend with in this life is our own ego, our shell-like identity, which has absorbed the nefarious negative programs of the old controllers and thus erroneously perceives itself to be under perpetual threat.

As the ego continues to pursue this survival driven way of being, it can get challenging to believe that that is not who we are. So therefore, the first step on our healing journey is to understand that if it's coming from the vibration of fear, it is a lie. And if it's coming from the vibration of love, it is the truth.

It takes a very brave soul to receive these words and run with them a very, very brave soul indeed. And it's my deepest prayer that those of you reading these words will understand that this is the path to deep, eternal, and perpetual healing because God is love, and our souls are made of love.

It is only in the third-dimensional temporary

holographic construct that we are programmed to experience this idea of threat and separation and in the absolute true reality, all is blissful, unified, and loving.

Therefore, when we practice discipline towards our egoic consciousness and choose to align with thoughts of love, comfort, and safety, we are very, very, very quickly rewarded on our spiritual path.

So that is the first fundamental step of healing our sexual trauma – attaining self-discipline with regards to being able to identify and ultimately transcend the narrative of the egoic consciousness.

The second step is finding a healing meditation practice.

Our consciousness can very much be likened to a hospital. The hospital is our mind, and so we must approach the healing of any trauma that we have experienced, be it emotional, physical, or sexual trauma from a psycho-spiritual level.

We must recognize that within our perfect imagination lies the "I-am-gination," remembering that God is referred to as "I AM" in the Bible. Within our imagination, we possess the ability to find resolution for traumatic experiences, completely rewrite the script, and craft a happy, forgiving, and liberating conclusion, with regards to traumatic events that we have experienced in the past be that in this lifetime or be that in previous lifetimes..

This is what I have done through working with Quantum Time Travel Therapy. I have literally gone back in time, comforted my inner child and given her what she needs.

I truly believe this is the mother of all healing modalities.

If you can find a way to identify the most traumatic moments in your life and in your mind's eye, travel back in time to see and meet that aspect and bring comfort to him or her, you will discover that very, very quickly you will heal all of your trauma at the deepest level.

You have the power to heal yourself recorrect yourself, and reconfigure yourself in alignment with your true, holy and divine blueprint.

Please see the accompanying workbook, where I share an inner child meditation, which will introduce you to working coherently and masterfully with healing your inner child.

Who knows whether the healing journey ever ends while we are in these bodies?

When we experience a traumatic incident in our life if we are not offered a safe space to talk it out release it and bring in Healing frequencies to this experience this experience gets lodged into our subconscious mind and it creates what could be termed a glitch or a knot.

The knot is representative of the fact that in The Subtle energetic realms, the flow of prana or chi energy must have to work through that Knot structure, and this therefore is not conducive to optimum well-being.

This is how trauma builds up in our energetic field ultimately, these Kinks and glitches lead to bad luck and repetition of negative situations and make us face our fears repetitively, therefore it is very important if we are on a spiritual path to understand that being born at this time in this society means automatically we have all been subjected to traumatic incidents and even when we have cleared our own personal trauma, very often our higher self will sign us up to heal our family trauma, our ancestral trauma, our karmic trauma, our past life trauma and our collective trauma – this is what I have had first-hand experience of…..

What I can say from my own personal experience is that I incarnated into a family that had very, very dark, heavy, complex sexual trauma knots.

In this trauma-healing work that I have done, I have experienced that everything is a frequency, and the pattern that was locked in my family karma held a particular resonant frequency, and through my spiritual journey and meeting and embodying my higher self, this higher frequency has been disrupted and has now fully dissolved the old knotted system.

Therefore, if it has worked for me, I know it will

work for you.

The benefits of inner child healing are:

Confidence,

Becoming more and more yourself,

Abundance,

Health,

Wellbeing,

Spiritual opportunities,

Doors opening for you,

Happiness,

Laughter,

Beautiful friendships.

So many benefits align when we heal these deep traumatic knots, be they from our own personal experience, our family's experience, or the collective experience.

I wish you the deepest love and support on your healing journey, and know that as you heal yourself, you heal all your past and future generations to come, to all our relations.

Aho Mitakuye Oyasin

CHAPTER 8

PORNOGRAPHY

In this chapter, I would like to devote a few paragraphs to speaking about pornography and how I perceive pornography from a spiritual perspectieve.

As we have covered in the previous chapter, things went down at the time of Atlantis, which ultimately caused Atlantis as a civilization to fall. Part of that was the control and manipulation of human DNA. This was done as a direct program attack through the fourth-dimensional moon matrix reincarnation loop. And this activated precisely what we have in our society to this day.

Part of that agenda, in my humble opinion, was to implement pornography as a dark web program into the consciousness template that humanity ultimately holds.

I believe that this was part of the old Atlantean controller's agenda, which was to control humanity and create a slave race of robots armed primarily with the ability to fulfil their enslaver's needs.

This is a very deep subject, and it was debatable whether I was going to bring this subject into this book. But as a genuine and authentic writer, I have always given my community the front-row insights I am experiencing in real-time from my spiritual team. And I understand that this is very, very high level information, which some of you may or may not be ready for, or resonate with.

In the book's concluding section, I will furnish resources for you to delve into the insights of some exceptional teachers with whom I've had the privilege to work. These teachers have played a role in guiding me to the conclusions I've shared.

It's crucial to note that my own awakening experience, atop a mountain which saw my third eye blasting open, led to the dissolution of my ego, and an ensuing merging of it with the vast ocean of God consciousness. While my recollections have primarily been an internal phenomenon, the past few years of my awakened journey have granted me the honour of meeting some of this planet's most esteemed spiritual teachers. I am pleased to provide their links for you at the end of this book.

So, back to pornography. It's my most profound understanding that pornography was designed and created by the nefarious overlords in order to create a society that would be dependent and driven by its lower base sexual nature.

At this point, I feel we must speak about the chakra system.

The human body comprises seven spinning chakra points, which is the physical earthly aspect of the chakra system. We, of course, have a 12-chakra system, a 15-chakra system, a 33-chakra system and a 144-chakra system. But the chakra system that is being spoken about in this book is the seven chakra system.

In the framework of the seven-chakra system, we encounter the base chakra. This chakra, situated where the genital organs and anus are, warrants discussion in these pages.

It is my profound understanding that humanity faces the choice of engaging in the lower base chakra stimulation aspects that our sexuality offers. While there is no judgment in that, I firmly believe that it is not the sole purpose of our incarnation to focus solely on stimulating our lower base chakra needs and desires. As we progress on our spiritual journey, we become more skilled at making choices from the heart space or even the vibration of the crown chakra. It's crucial to recognize that these choices fundamentally resonate at a different vibrational level than those made purely from the base level.

This discussion is intricately linked to pornography and the agenda of the old controllers. We have all been provided with a choice – whether to succumb to the impulses and desires rooted in the lower aspects of our nature. The decisions we make determine whether we will yield to these urges or rise above them through wisdom and practice, elevating our sexual drives and inclinations to a more heart-centred and enlightened level.

In my perspective, pornography has been wielded as a spiritual weapon to be used against humanity.

My understanding is that when we pass over in these vessels, either bringing these vessels with us or leaving them behind, it is my deepest understanding that when we die, we're not met by a judgmental God-like figure. We are met by our own eternal angelic Christ self who will assist us to look fairly upon all of the choices we made in that lifetime from a deeply spiritual perspective.

If we made choices in our life that were not in alignment with our highest expression, we will ourselves decide to return back to the third dimensional experience in order to make more higher enlightened Godly choices.

We are all evolving to our highest, purest, angelic aspect, and no one judges us except our own higher self. And we are judged from a place of love as a parent would look upon a child.

So, I believe that this is a realm where we are given free will and the freedom to make choices.

Because of my spiritual awakening experiences, I found that from a very young age, I surrendered my ego and my ego's needs and desires and dedicated my life to the mantra "thy will, not my will."

And I repeated this mantra all day every day because

I didn't want to live my life from my egoic will.

I wanted to become one with my higher self absolutely, and it was natural for me to assert that God's will, my higher self's will, was the steerer of this earthly consciousness ship.

So, in my humble opinion pornography is a weapon used to tempt and lure beautiful, exquisite humanity to make choices that are going to keep them entrapped in lower physical beastly vibrations.

The sexually enticing energies of pornography are very intense and magnetic, and they can easily cause one to forget to focus on one's spiritual development, causing one to get lost spiritually due to the addictive habits and patterns that are born of chasing low-base level stimulation and experiences.

So, if you are reading these words, it is my deepest prayer that you will wake up to the nefarious agenda of pornography and never consume pornography again. My prayer is that you will see it as the spiritual weapon that has been used against beautiful humanity.

No longer will you put yourself in the firing line to receive this destructive war-like agenda. You will remember your holiness. You will remember you're a child of God, and that you hold that God energy within you. And in this remembrance, it's my deepest prayer that you repeat the mantra "Not my will, but thy will be done."

My prayer is that you surrender your life to your higher self, your God self. And make choices that your higher self will be so thankful for and proud of you for making.

CHAPTER 9

WHITE TANTRA

In this chapter, I would like to speak about the path of white Tantra. Traditionally speaking, White Tantra refers to the path of semen retention 100% of the time. Grey Tantra is partly retaining the semen in sexual intercourse, and black Tantra is releasing the semen in sexual intercourse.

The path of black Tantra is not a topic I will delve deeply into in this book. However, I will mention that it is closely linked to the exaltation and reverence of the lowest, lustful, beastly, addictive, and insatiable aspects of human nature, which are inherent in our animalistic sexual nature.

There has been a considerable agenda to normalize what could be termed black tantra or the path of non-sacred sexuality. And that is exactly what we, in the West, have been exposed to, particularly in the last 50 years.

But where my heart lies is to speak about the white tantric path, as this is a subject that I hold so dearly in my heart. As I write these words, I see two etheric swans doing a mating dance in front of me. And I know intuitively that this is a sign from my higher self telling me that this symbol truly represents the white tantric path.

The white tantric path is the path of recognition. Recognition of one's holy self, recognition of one's holy sexual nature, recognition of the holy sexual creative powers one has been bestowed with, and recognition of the fact that one's sacred sexual energy must not be shared with anyone other than a loving soul contracted beloved.

Part of white Tantra is recognizing that your beloved is an embodiment of the Christ self – your beloved is God's holy son or God's holy daughter.

The white tantric path recognizes that the Phallus and the yoni of your beloved is the most extraordinary symbol of divinity and must be adored and revered.

I believe that the white tantric path is deeply connected to new-earth sexuality. And I believe that this is connected to the Atlantean values that we held as a collective consciousness at the time of Atlantis prior to the fall.

I deeply believe that we are evolving back to this place whereby we hold our sexuality in perpetual reverence individually and collectively, and as we anchor the new earth sexuality codes, it is my deepest intuitive knowing that we will return back to the practice whereby when a soul incarnates, their birth chart will be looked over by a mystical astrologer who will be able to tell them the exact timeline of meeting their beloved divine counterpart, and we will all live in a culture whereby we prepare ourselves physically, emotionally, spiritually, and sexually, to be with this ultimate tantric twin counterpart.

We will return back to the knowing and understanding that we are not here to share our sexual energy with just anyone. Our sexuality and sexual energy must be honoured and revered for the sacred energy that it truly is.

It is my deepest understanding and inner standing that in that vibration of recognition, all temptations that were born from the black tantric path will be obliterated and annihilated at their root.

The white tantric path is the path of the priest and the priestess, and holds the recognition of the fact that each sexual encounter is an encounter of the God and the Goddess of creation, coming together to consummate ecstatic love within the universe and multiverse.

The path of white Tantra is the path of sexual devotion, sexual adoration, sexual ecstasy, sexual bliss, sexual freedom, and sexual alignment with the highest sexuality path.

This is not the space to talk about sexual positions and practices.

Although in my accompanying workbook, I do share some white tantric sexual practices.

It is my deepest prayer that humanity awakens to what has been going on with the nefarious programming around our sexuality and wake up to the realization that pornography, OnlyFans, prostitution, polyamory etc., all these ways are serving the black and the grey hand path.

And it is my deepest prayer that more and more people will awaken to who we truly are as fractals of God source energy – Holy Saints and avatars who have returned back to fully actualize and awaken in these physical vessels.

I have been inspired by some very great teachers on my journey of understanding the path of white tantra and sacred sexuality – teachers such as Thomas T Burgoyne and Samael Aun Weor have been particularly instrumental and inspirational for me with regard to deepening my knowledge in this subject matter.

This is what Samael Aun Weor says about semen retention from the book "The Perfect Matrimony":

"It is not necessary to spill the semen to engender a child. Imbeciles like to spill the semen. The gnostic is not an imbecile. When the couples are sexually united, clairvoyants usually see a very brilliant light which envelopes the pair. In this instant precisely, the creative of man comes to serve as means for the creation of a new being.

"When the couple allows themselves to be carried

away by carnal passions, and then commit the crime of spilling the seeds, those luminous forces withdraw.

"Their place is taken by Luciferic forces of a blood red colour, bringing quarrels, jealousy, adultery, tears and desperation to the home."

"This is how homes which could have been a heaven on earth become true infernos. Whoever does not spill the semen, retains and accumulates for himself peace, abundance, wisdom, happiness and love.

"With the key to sexual magic, one can put an end to disputes in the home. This is the key to true happiness. During the act of sexual magic, couples are charged with magnetism. They magnetize each other. The pelvis of the woman pours out feminine currents while the breasts give off masculine ones. In the man, the feminine current is rooted in the mouth and the masculine in his virile member. All these organs should be well excited by means of sexual magic in order to give and receive, transmit and collect vital magnetic forces, and continue increasing extraordinarily in quantity and quality.

"In the homes of gnostic initiates where between the couple there is such intimate sexual contact, delightful dance, joyful music and ardent kiss have the object of achieving the mutual magnetization of man and woman.

"The magnetic power is masculine and feminine at

the same time. The man needs the currents of his wife if he really wants to progress. And inevitably, she needs those of her husband to achieve the development of her powers.

"When the couples magnetize each other, things progress and happiness makes its nest in the home. When a man and woman unite, something is created. Scientific chastity permits the transmutation of the sexual secretions into light and fire.

"Every religion which degenerates preaches celibacy. Even every religion at its birth and in its glorious splendour preaches the path of the perfect matrimony."

I was guided to share these powerful words and introduce you to the perfect Matrimony book I highly recommend checking out the bibliography at the back of the book whereby I share some very interesting and amazing books that have been instrumental in bringing forth this book.

CHAPTER 10

HOLY SEXUALISM

As a continuation from this extraordinary topic of white tantra and delving deep into the great mystical Teachings of the Perfect Matrimony I was guided by my spiritual team to dig deep into my written transmission archives and pull through relevant articles that I have shared on this particular subject matter.

This chapter includes one of these articles, and it is on the subject theme of holy sexualism. I am very drawn to add this chapter to this book, as part of the essence of this book is to offer a brand new yet deeply ancient approach to our sexuality so that we may step out of the dark beastly toxic programming that has been enforced upon beautiful humanity through the media through the dark web, through films which have normalised multiple sexual partners, etc.

We have all grown up with the belief that this is natural and this is normal without having any understanding of the energetic implications that we each experience every time we merge intimately with another soul, be that through sexual intercourse or even simply through kissing another person. As mentioned previously in this book, the saliva contains an energetic map of every soul that we have connected with sexually, and if we have not worked to cleanse and purify these energies they will stay locked into our subtle energetic field causing all manner of chaos and havoc...

There are so many variations of sexuality these days: pansexual, bisexual, heterosexual etc. None of those labels has ever resonated for me because it is just so dualistic to put oneself into a category, but if I were to choose a category I deeply resonate with I would choose holy-sexual. Now I would like to talk about holy-sexualism...

How about we all affirm, "I am holy sexual."

Maybe collectively, we could start a movement whereby hetero/homo sexualism can be upgraded to holy sexualism – where one only desires to mate and experience an energetic connection with a soul who also recognises the holiness of one's sacred sexuality and one's whole being. Holy sexualism understands the codes of devotion and self-love and understands that we all hold the holy flame within us, meaning that when our higher self aligns us with a sacred beloved, we recognise the holy Christed self that dwells within them.

We remember that it is our sacred responsibility, bestowed upon us by God, to love others in the manner God would wish to love them if God were present on this earth. With this understanding, we cherish and honour them, nurturing a bond of commitment and loyalty. Our approach to sexuality is imbued with deep devotion and reverence, recognizing its profound sacredness within the context of our relationships and interactions with others.

In holy sexual relationships, there is an altar whereby we offer gratitude to the spiritual realms for our sacred love and union. And we offer roses regularly to the altar of our sacred sexuality to keep all our holy sexual juices flowing. We do deep meditations together. We lie together in the great stillness, experience deep tantric intercourse, energetic clearings of the highest order, and the transmutation and alchemy of one's most extraordinary shadow aspect.

Holy sexualism is deeply connected to the core belief that we have a high-level spiritual partner chosen by our creator, mother, father God, with whom we have made a soul contract to be with in this lifetime.

This path of holy sexualism understands implicitly that each partnership that we experience before that sacred union is preparation for that ultimate union with the ultimate God mate that our soul is contracted to journey with, in this lifetime.

CHAPTER 11

HEALING OUR PERCEPTION / OUR SIGHT TO RECOGNIZE THE HOLINESS OF OUR SEXUALITY.

In this chapter, I would like to share some deep esoteric wisdom pertaining to the third eye chakra and how this relates to the fulfilment of our greatest sexual spiritual potential...

There is a very important reason why our ancient ancestors, such as the Egyptians and Mayans, were so profoundly obsessed with the pineal gland.

Our ancient ancestors were well aware that whatever we perceive is exactly what we call in and create in our physical reality, and reality is not happening out there per se; it happens from within and is shaped by our "perception".

Reality is a mirror and manifestation of our innermost perception, therefore, a huge amount of healing of our sexuality is related to healing our perception and understanding the spiritual power we hold as we perceive our beloved.

On my spiritual awakening journey, I quickly understood that I, as a divine feminine, have been endowed with the divine mother codes, and that means that I am highly adept and able to birth my own divine self out of this secular paradigm back into the sacred paradigm.

It became very clear to me as I birthed and anchored my own divine Holy self that my beloved's spiritual liberation was deeply connected to the purification and cleansing of my perception, which either saw him as a third-dimensional being or as the true divine holy being that he truly, truly is.

I quickly awakened to the realization that I held an enormous responsibility as the divine feminine and that as I held my divine masculine with the eyes of purity, innocence, and perpetual divinity, this was sacred nourishment that was allowing the seed of his divine Christed self to blossom and become the fruit – the potential of his beautiful divine self.

This is deeply connected to all aspects of our spiritual evolutionary process, but I would like to speak about this, particularly in the area of sacred sexuality.

If you are a female reading these words, please understand how much power you hold.

In the Rider Waite tarot, we are explicitly shown that the high priestess is the second card in the deck, and in this card we see that she's holding the book of knowledge, the Torah, and the book is open. This is symbolic of the fact that she has been deemed less corruptible than the divine masculine with regard to being a recipient of divine knowledge and wisdom.

These teachings vividly illustrate the responsibility of the divine feminine to purify her perception and nurture her eternal innocence. Once accomplished, she gains the ability to hold space and maintain the ideal perception of her divine masculine counterpart. This enables his divine essence to emerge away from secularism, and anchor into the eternal truth of his perpetual divinity.

Therefore, we must speak about the importance of the pineal gland with regard to atoning our sexuality and leveraging our sexuality codes back to a place of paradise, which is where they ultimately belong.

If you are a divine feminine reading these words, it is my deepest prayer that you take responsibility for your spiritual power and that you birth your own divine innocence through the recognition that you are an aspect of God source energy and you are a daughter of our infinite creator.

You are endowed with all of the creative and spiritual powers of our divine creator, and as you birth and anchor your own divinity, it is my deepest prayer that when your divine beloved steps into your field, you are able to recognize him as the perpetually innocent son of God that he truly is.

May you remember that through your eyes, you are able to assist him on the deepest level. Through your perception of him, you are able to literally walk him home out of the material realm, back to the spiritual realms.

Through your perception, you are able to offer your divine beloved the greatest gift that words cannot possibly comprehend.

You are able to hold his sexual innocence in your deepest heart core, and through this perception, you are able to restore him back to his original spiritual divine pattern. As all of the hermetic teachings clearly remind us – whatever it is that we see and perceive is exactly what we are magnetizing and drawing into our physical reality. So, if we can see our beloved as the Christed being that he is, these are the necessary vibrational codes which will transform his spiritual vibration and anchor him fully in his highest Godly potential.

Our sexuality is such a profound gift that has been given to us by our God self.

It is where so much of our power can be sourced, and this is why there has been so much manipulation and control with regard to humanity's sexuality.

There has been such a huge agenda to activate a corruption of the blueprint/patterning of our sacred sexuality to ensure that we come to the false conclusions, that we are not innocent and we are underserving of the sweetest love that is available in the multiverse.

Dearest one reading these words, please know that you were created for the sweetest, most powerful love in the universe, but it comes down to you and what you will allow into your energetic field and the choices that you make in this lifetime.

If you continue to consume porn, open relationships, polyamory, and all manner of sexually loose actions, then in my humble opinion, you are simply holding up your evolutionary process and you will stay stuck in the reincarnation loop until you make choices that are in alignment with the vibrations of your beautiful higher self.

There is so much to speak about on this subject matter, and I will continue to weave in this topic throughout the remaining chapters of this book.

CHAPTER 12

HOW DO WE WORSHIP THE LINGAM?

In this chapter, we will approach the extraordinarily beautiful yet somehow very sensitive subject of how we worship the Lingam.

By now, hopefully, the words from the previous chapters are working their magic and your consciousness is opening like a lotus flower and blossoming in receivership of these words, and they are triggering an ancient, holy, knowing and remembrance within you that you are a priestess, that you are a priest, that you are an aspect of Christ-consciousness, Jen the Christ, John the Christ, Bob the Christ, Carol the Christ etc.

We are all embodiments of that sacred, divine being.

Embracing our true nature naturally leads to the recognition that our fellow beings, our brothers and sisters, are external reflections of ourselves, originating from the same identical source energy.

As we stand in ecstatic recognition and celebration of both ourselves and others, we immerse ourselves in the vibration of union. This vibration of union serves as the code through which we encounter the lingam, or the phallus, aligning with our own eternal, divine higher self and experiencing union with our beloved.

In this sacred union, his divine member serves as a perfect reflection of his masculine spiritual essence. This recognition causes our sacred sight to be healed and ensures the dusty remnants of sleep and forgetfulness be cleansed from our inner perception.

It is now that we see and recognize the divine masculine and his Lingam for what they truly are, for what stands before you or as you is the masculine aspect of God himself.

The aspect of consciousness that was brave enough to burst out of the spiritual realms, to experience the illusion of separation from all that is in order to have the experience of living as spirit as matter.

With our inner and outer eyes cleansed, we understand the vulnerability of the divine masculine and that the phallus was given as a rope that, when he held it, would connect him instantly with his holy, divine, eternal self.

He would feel safe when he held his phallus. He would feel held, he would feel home. And this was the gift that God gave him, to somehow remind him that he is never truly alone.

When we perceive the phallus in this way with these white tantric eyes that recognize the vulnerability and ecstatic beauty that it represents, then the only natural way to meet the phallus is to bow with one's hands together.

It would then be appropriate to make offerings to the

phallus, offerings of touch, offerings of oil, offerings of falling red rose petals.

The way to honour the phallus is to be grateful for it, to say thank you for everything that it holds and is.

This is how we worship the phallus.

CHAPTER 13

HOW TO IMPLEMENT LINGAM WORSHIP INTO YOUR CURRENT RELATIONSHIP.

If you are blessed to have vibrationally aligned with this information, then in my humble opinion, you are one of the leaders in this sexual revolution.

This is the revolution that takes sex out of the base chakra and integrates it with the higher crown chakra to ultimately meet in the very centre of the heart chakra.

These teachings hold within them the deepest essence of tantric love making.

These teachings are anchored in the vibration of unconditional true love, a love that has been contracted to take place and has been heralded by the spiritual realms as a union of great importance for this time.

These teachings are the foundation of the tantric merge that takes place in a tantric union.

Exposure to these teachings enables you fully to outgrow the programming and tendency to shop around as well as the soul-degrading habit of swiping left and right for the next hook up.

Instead, these teachings drop you right into the heart space and enable you to focus on your own spiritual intensity and magnetism to ultimately attract your heart's sacred beloved into your energetic field.

Therefore, if you feel deeply inspired to bring this practice into your current relationship, let's look at a few ways to make this happen.

The first and foremost way is to create a sacred sexual altar in the space where you make love and are intimately connect with your beloved.

This altar could have pictures of tantric Union, This altar could have red velvet, roses, candles, and crystals that are associated with sacred sexuality: indeed, whatever objects deeply inspire you to get your sexual juices flowing.

The next step would be to focus on the aroma in the space as the nose has such a huge part to play in terms of sexual arousal. There are some scents that are associated with sexual arousal and pleasure, and some of these are Ylang-ylang, Frankincense, Myrrh, Spikenard, Rose, Galbanum, Angelica, Blue Tansey, Blue Lotus, Lily, and Cedarwood.

In order to create your sacred space to experience Lingam worship, it would be advisable to have the scents either burning away in the form of incense, or steaming away in a diffuser.

The third step would be to create a very, very comfortable, luscious, beautiful, sacred space for you and your divine counterpart to connect on a tantric level.

The next stage would be to set a date for this sensual tantric meeting one great suggestion is to utilize the potency of numerology and working with cosmic numbers. You could choose a time and a date such as 2:22 or 11:11 or 10:10 to converge.

When we mark the moment numerologically, this adds a profoundly powerful intensity to the meet and merge of you and your divine beloved at the appointed time.

When it's time, I would invite you to both sit on your blankets or comfortable cushions that you have created in your alter space, and I would invite you to decide whether you wish to be naked initially or not.

Once you have made that decision, (many beloveds will choose to be naked) assuming that is the choice that you have made, It is highly advisable that you look into the tantric position, the Yab Yum, which is where the man sits in a cross-legged position, and the woman sits atop him with her legs wrapped around him.

This is a way to ensure that all of the chakras touch, merge, align and attune to each other's divine sexual frequency.

I would highly recommend starting with simple eye gazing without words, – just really deeply looking into your beloved's eyes, and I would hold this practice for a minimum of five minutes, maximum of 20 minutes, even up to one hour.

I would then gently start using touch in a consensual way to start bringing in the frequencies of arousal, sensuality, and pleasure.

After some time, I would then invite my beloved to lie down, and I would invite him to relax deeply, and I would make sure that the space is very, very warm with either a fire burning or a heater.

I would invite him to lie down naked, and I would have lots of rose petals in a bowl next to me, and I would start gently dropping the rose petals on his holy phallus member from about a meter above him.

I would do this for about five or ten minutes while chanting the mantra OM coupled with repeating phrases such as, "You are safe now". "You are home". "You are safe now. Welcome home." "You are safe now."

This is a very, very powerful mantra to use when approaching the practice of Lingam worship.

I would then, with my beloved divine masculine's permission, anoint him with sacred rose oil that is mixed with a base of coconut oil, which is very, very gentle and nourishing for the phallus area.

I would have the oil slightly heated, and I would very, very gently start pouring drops of oil onto the phallus area, and once the area has been saturated with the oil, I would then gently caress the phallus and massage out all the excess oil.

I would then ask him if he would like to receive more Lingam massage.

In my accompanying Workbook I share more in-depth information on the intricacies of Lingam massage.

I would then wipe the remainder of the oil with a really soft, gentle towel, and then I would invite my beloved to receive an almond milk and scented rose phallus bathe.

At this point I would have a chair ready and invite him to sit on the chair as I performed the abhishekam. In the appendix of this book, I share more in-depth information about abhishekam.

As I pour the milky elixir over his phallus, I would ask him to visualize all of his sexual trauma, guilt and shame washing away.

I would ask him to place all of his guilt, fear, and shame with regards to his sexuality in a black box, and I would ask him to visualize this black box being burnt away with a violet flame.

I would then ask him to visualize this box washing away and as the milky substance washes away and cleanses his phallus member, so too will all his burdens and all his troubles be washed away.

I would again wipe the phallus dry, and then I would

finally offer some blessed spring water that had been warmed. I would then finally pour with a beautiful chalice, warm spring-water on his divine Phallus member, and I would ask him to visualize all past lives, all karmic ties all collective masculine associations with guilt, fear and dominance with regards to masculine sexuality, and I would ask him to devote this final cleanse to clearing this out at the root.

As the final drops of water goes onto the phallus, we would both visualize the root of personal and collective sexual shame, disgust and fear being prized out at the deepest root level.

This is a basic outline of a Lingam worship/anointing practice.

It is my deepest hope and prayer that this inspires you to curate your own profoundly beautiful ceremony.

There is no right or wrong.

The intention with which we must approach the ceremony must be reverence, forgiveness, and deep compassion for the role that the divine masculine has taken on as God's frontline Shiva warriors.

What can you add to this list?

What really, really deeply inspires you that you would like to share with your beloved?

Please know that in my workbook that accompanies

this book, I share this practice in somewhat more depth and intricacy.

The way that we approach the Lingam is through our healed perception and our heart-based consciousness, which understands exactly what the divine masculine consciousness has gone through in order to physicalize out of the oneness of the spiritual realms into the maya, the illusion of duality.

The divine masculine has been coded to take the brunt of the dualistic experiment and is therefore worthy of profound devotion and cherishment.

This is how we worship the Lingam by recognizing and deepening our love and empathy towards the divine masculine, appreciating on a deep level who he is and the role that he has played out on a spiritual level to be incarnated in this physical vessel at this time.

CHAPTER 14

HOW TO START A NEW RELATIONSHIP WHICH INCLUDES LINGAM WORSHIP.

In this chapter, I would like to cover the subject matter of initiating a new relationship and introducing Lingam worship into this new relationship.

In the previous chapter, I have shared a succinct outline of a Lingam worship/anointing practice, and this can be applied to your relationship, whatever stage you are in.

In this chapter, I aim to address the specific conversations that are important for us to have with our intimate partners as we transition from the programmed, secular model of sexuality to the sacred divine model of sexuality.

The first thing that I would suggest upon meeting a new beloved is to establish whether they resonate with the idea of experiencing a sacred relationship.

If the person in front of you says no, they do not resonate with that, then I would really deeply invite you to question whether you are vibrationally matched.

But I'm sure that everyone reading these words will

be attracting into their lives divine beloveds who have also received the memo regarding only engaging in sacred relationships.

Therefore, if you are starting a brand new relationship and you want to introduce Lingam practice into it, then it may be a really good idea to recommend this book to your sacred partner as a good starting ground and explain that you have been familiarized with these teachings, and they resonate with you. Then share that you would like to introduce this practice into your sacred relationship.

If you are a man who has aligned with these powerful tantric teachings, then my deepest suggestion to you is pray to the universe/ your higher self/ your soul consciousness, to send you the perfect woman, the perfect divine goddess who is a vibrational match to these teachings.

If you have come across these powerful teachings and are ready to run with this and make it part of your life and reality, then you absolutely deserve a partner / a sacred beloved who is able to work with you in this deeply sacred and beautiful way.

If you are a woman, then exactly the same thing. Drop into meditation, drop into no mind. Understand that mind is simply of the temporal realm, No mind is of the eternal realms, step into no mind. And then from that place, ask the universe / your higher self-consciousness to send you a perfect partner who's ready to go forward and implement these teachings.

It's very important that we understand that this manual holds very old, ancient knowledge that has been kept hidden from humanity, but now in this age, we are remembering that we are the priest and the priestess who have incarnated to bring back and live out this ancient information. And that is what this book is dedicated to.

Dear women that are reading this book, I'm sure there will be a sequel at some point called yoni worship because of course, the yoni must also be worshipped since the yoni is the portal of birth that births souls from the spiritual realms into the physical realms.

So of course, there will be a book whereby we go into great depth with regards to yoni worship teachings.

What a deeply exciting journey that we are all on. And I'm so grateful that I received these remembrances whilst on the Holy Mountain of Arunachala, and I'm so grateful for Lord Shiva and all of the darkness that I experienced, which through Shiva's grace, I was able to transmute into the most exquisitely beautiful light I have ever beheld.

And for that, I am so very, very grateful. And I'm grateful to every single one of you who holds this book in your hands and holds these beautiful teachings deep in the centre of your core. And who are now committed avidly to pursuing the sacred practice of Lingam worship.

CHAPTER 15

WHY DO WE WORSHIP THE LINGAM?

We worship the Lingam because the Lingam is worthy of being worshiped. It has taken a lot of courage for the Lingam to come into physical form. It has taken a great deal of passion power and divine masculine force for the Lingam to be here now. And the Lingam belongs to the masculine aspect of the Godself. For so long, man has been portrayed as the violent warrior. God himself has been portrayed as predominantly the violent murderer.

This has all been an agenda to bastardize and corrupt the divine template of who the divine masculine is. And we as a collective consciousness have had enough.

We call now for the ending of this bombardment of lies that came about through conditioning and programming.

This is not our truth.

The truth is:

The divine masculine is beautiful.

The divine masculine is holy.

The divine masculine is sacred.

The divine masculine is God's son.

The divine masculine is God himself.

The divine masculine is God.

The divine masculine is love.

The divine masculine is power.

And that is why the divine masculine is worthy to receive deep reverence and honour towards his sacred member in sexual relationships and intimacy.

In my humble opinion, it is time that we all collectively acknowledge the sacred magical power that the divine masculine holds. And this book is dedicated to that.

This book is a seed that many, many souls will receive. And each soul who reads this book will experience the flowering of their own recognition and remembrance of the divine masculine.

As a divine feminine, the remembrance will come with the deep compulsion to honour and revere the sacred phallus member which our beloved possesses, and as the divine masculine, if you are reading these words, this is an opportunity to own your divinity, to allow the tears to come, because these words will absolutely trigger tears. And those tears will break down the programming. The tears will break down the walls the mind has built to protect itself from this ugly matrix construct.

Everyone reading these words will collectively orchestrate a great turning of the wheel of human consciousness, moving us back towards the sacred and out of the secular.

And this is why we worship the Lingam. We worship the Lingam because the Lingam is worthy of receiving devotion.

When we approach the Lingam, it is very important that we approach it with softness and presence, tenderness and strength, the strength of our own priestess power, that finally, we have awoken to what it truly means to revere the phallus.

We approach the Lingam through awakening to the remembrance of the torturous battle scars, the divine masculine soul consciousness has experienced as he led the way out of the spiritual realms into this physical external world of matter.

We worship the Lingam because we are transforming as a society, as a collective consciousness, to a society which recognizes the truth of God in every breath, in every hair, in every grain of sand.

A society which recognizes God in every smile, in every song, in every leaf that blows.

When we remember this truth collectively, we will all know great, great ecstasy.

The ecstasy that our ancient ancestors knew who

walked this earth before us. And we will restore this earth back to its original paradisical state.

We are the generation who have come forth from the highest spiritual realms to make this happen.

It is happening now as we awaken to the old programming agenda.

We release the old out dated and expired nefarious programming through working with the violet flame of transmutation, which empowers and enables us to step forward, empty, clear, and spacious in full knowing and recognition of our inherent divine identity.

CHAPTER 16

WORKING WITH THE VIOLET FLAME

In this book, I have presented a revival of an old tantric healing practice that is depicted in many of the temples in beautiful India. And in bringing forth this information, I have shared about the necessity to meet and face our shadow self and let go of the programming that does not belong to us or serve us. This powerful reminder has been echoed throughout many, many pages in this book, and therefore, I feel it would not be complete if I did not share with you a most exceptionally powerful tool that has been given to us by the ascended higher consciousness of light, in order to assist us to rapidly progress in this threshold ascension lifetime, a gift that brings us great power and potency – to work with the violet flame.

Many of you reading these words will be already familiar with the violet flame and will have been working with it for many, many years. However, if you have never heard of the violet flame, please allow me to introduce the violet flame.

Within our higher dimensional reality, we have many ascended beings. One of those ascended beings is called St. Germaine.

St. Germaine has been given the auspicious duty of being the guardian of the violet flame. The violet flame was given to humanity in order to transmute the dark energies that would inevitably arise at the time of Kali Yuga, which is now ending, and which we are rapidly coming out of.

The gift of the violet flame has brought with it the understanding that we have the power to hold anything in our mind's eye that we wish to let go of. The technique is to see this thought / programme/ belief in the centre of the violet flame and being consumed by the violet flame.

The power of just simply seeing the violet flame transmuting our intention would be enough to erase it out of the Akashic records forever and ever.

On my spiritual awakening path, I have worked profusely with the violet flame and it has always assisted me and accelerated my spiritual mastery process.

In my accompanying workbook, I share a very, very high level guided meditation that will enable you to have a direct experience of working with the violet flame.

The great teachers, Mark and Claire Prophet, brought through in their mystery school powerful reminders of the energy of St. Germaine and the transmissions that he brought forth. And I love and honour them for the spiritual work that they have done, particularly with regards to bringing forth the truth about the violet flame, at this time.

Please see the resources at the back of the book with links to their work.

CHAPTER 17

WHAT HAPPENS IN OUR LIFE WHEN WE WORSHIP THE LINGAM?

This is a vast subject area, and, in many ways, reaching a point of worshipping the Lingam represents a significant advancement along the path of our evolution.

When we arrive at this place, we open ourselves up to receive a profound transformation in our energetic frequency. This transformation has a huge effect on our life specifically with regards to our own personal subjective experiences.

When I awakened to this divine, ancient tantric truth and fell to my knees in devotion towards the holy phallus and all that it represents, I immediately noticed that the most exquisite divine masculines started being magnetized into my energetic field.

Every time I went out, I would align with an angelic masculine who was very tapped in on the spiritual level and could see and recognize me as the tantrika that I am.

In the subtle plains of my reality, I experienced a profound interchange of reverence between myself and these divine masculine souls who miraculously found themselves in my energetic field.

After this awakening process, which happened a lot while I was in India, I found that everywhere I looked, the universe was sending me, or I should say, I was aligning with, extraordinarily beautiful divine masculine souls. This was an extraordinary experience to behold and it was testimony to the efficacy of this shift in consciousness.

If you're in a relationship and embrace this tantric truth, you'll likely witness the clearing and transformation of many of your shadow aspects. This transformation can translate into heightened spiritual power, a deeper sense of belonging, increased success, enhanced magnetism, abundance, and numerous fortunate opportunities flowing into your life.

This journey embodies the divine sexual path of both masculine and feminine energies. This path has been hidden from humanity for aeons, but it is time now that this ancient truth returns to the mainstream, and we understand the power that is available to us when we approach the sacred phallus, the sacred Lingam, in this reverent way.

So many enormous gifts come forth when we awaken to Lingam worship.

As a man. If you are blessed enough to have a beloved who is awakened to the power of Lingam worship, this will activate a very, very deep healing process for you. And no doubt, this will trigger many elements of your shadow consciousness whereby you have stored shame, guilt, and avoidance around the expression of your full sexual power.

This level of presence and devotion will start dislodging those remnant shadow patterns, and please understand that this may be uncomfortable initially.

It's recommended that you ground yourself, stay hydrated, and recognize that you're engaged in a process that will profoundly impact your entire lineage, spanning seven generations back and seven generations forward.

This role as a recipient of the Lingam worship protocol will undoubtedly have a remarkable effect on our collective relationship with sexuality.

In other words, this is no mean feat. What you are doing is so huge and so important, particularly for the generations to come – we are literally birthing the new earth sexuality codes.

We are the vanguards who are leading the way out of this old third dimensional, superficially obsessed paradigm into the new spiritually evolved ecstatic earth. Therefore, as we experience these new protocols and codes in our lives, it is understandable that this will activate a cleansing and a purging of all of the programs, patterns and beliefs pertaining to the old vibration.

This is a path for the spiritual warriors. This is a path for the Shiva and the Shaktis, the Krishna, and the Radharanis. This is the path for awakened humanity who understand that we are the return of the gods and the goddesses.

This is the path of divine sexuality, the form of sexuality that was performed in the ancient tantric temples of India and many Eastern countries.

There are so many gifts that are born of this ancient tantric practice. I look forward to receiving all the beautiful messages that come from everyone who reads this book, sharing with me the gifts that they have experienced from committing to and living this spiritual practice.

CHAPTER 18

LINGAM, WORSHIP AND SACRED RELATIONSHIPS.

In this chapter, I would like to discuss how practising Lingam worship will affect those of us in current relationships.

As expressed in the previous paragraphs, Lingam worship is a high-level spiritual practice that can be likened to implementing a brand new frequency into one's energetic field.

Suppose there are lower frequencies pertaining to patterns of shame, disgust, embarrassment, etc. In that case, once this high frequency practice is introduced into the energetic field, this will activate a collapse of many old energies that have kept the old patterns and templates in place.

This can be a very confronting experience for those who are just starting out on their spiritual path, and it's highly advisable that you go easy on yourself whilst you are upgrading your sexuality codes. If you are not in a relationship and you are familiarized with these powerful teachings, then most likely this will affect your magnetism and the type of souls that you attract into your energetic field.

Suppose for example you are a heterosexual woman

reading this book and receiving these teachings most likely you will notice an upgrade in the men who are vibrationally aligned with you, and you will notice a huge number of divine masculines being deeply and profoundly magnetized into your energetic field.

This is a natural byproduct of upgrading our sexuality and introducing these sexuality protocols, either in relationships or if even if we are not in an intimate relationship.

This is a huge subject area to speak about, and many people will have an entire myriad of experiences dependent on their own perception and beliefs.

This is not a "one size fits all."

As we discussed earlier, our third eye plays a crucial role in our evolution and how we view humanity. What we perceive through it shapes what we see in our physical world.

Lingam worship is the new paradigm, sexuality path, and is deeply connected to ancient tantric teachings which often depict women as the leaders in tantra.

I take this to mean that women are the leaders in terms of birthing their own divine sexual innocence, and as this is birthed, they are thus able to perceive the eternal innocence of their divine masculine.

If you have been blessed to receive the teachings from this powerful book, it is my deepest prayer that you apply these teachings and principles and you practice Lingam worship either with a Shiva Lingam or with your beloved partner.

In my accompanying workbook, I share many tools, techniques and practices that can be done with or without a sexual partner.

These words are powerful enough to activate a powerful sexual awakening.

We are vanguarding a sexual spiritual revolution. We are leading the way out of the mundane, out of the debased elements of sexuality, and we are restoring our sacred sexuality back to the pristine level of God source energy.

It's important that we understand that this is not a sex manual. This is a tantric teaching that is being shared with humanity, with the intention to upgrade our sexuality codes and deliver them out of the mundane and back to the sacred.

In my accompanying workbook, I share practices, protocols, and techniques that you can apply to your relationship that will enable you to work on a very, very deep, practical level with these teachings. However, it is important to note that this book is simply the philosophy behind these tantric teachings.

It is important to remember that the divine feminine has been encoded through her purity and original divine template, to be deeply devoted to the Lingam.

We have all held these eternal truths within the

Akashic records, our own subconscious field. But as we all incarnate and interface with the fourth dimensional moon matrix reincarnation loop, many of these ancient truths become hidden, distorted, and unavailable for us to access before our incarnation and ensuing physicalization as spirit into matter.

The spiritual path is deeply connected to removing the veil that the nefarious programming has sought to inflict upon beautiful humanity so that we may bask in the eternal spiritual truth, which is our divine birthright.

Therefore, it's important to note that the divine feminine is encoded to hold deep reverence towards the sacred phallus because she is well aware of the journey that the divine masculine soul has taken to incarnate from the spiritual realms into the physical world of matter.

She is encoded to be his nurturer, his soother, his beloved, who bestows infinite pleasure, comfort, and deep security to him through his sacred sexuality.

It is time now for the divine feminine to fully, fully awaken to her original divine goddess self so that she may be able to offer the divine masculine, the love and support that he deeply needs in order to thrive in this material world.

We can create paradise on earth, but this can only happen if we all awaken deeply on a spiritual level and step out of the mundane programming that has sought to vilify humanity and attribute us with labels such as abused abuser, et cetera, et cetera.

CHAPTER 19

WOMEN ARE THE LEADERS IN TANTRA

This is a very, very deep subject, which I have covered extensively in my book "Twin Flames and the Event". I highly recommend reading this signature work that I have presented, as so many of the questions and terms which you may have been asking about from the present book will be made explicitly clear for you in "Twin Flames and the Event."

So that would be a very, very good foundational introduction to New Earth sexuality, fifth-dimensional relationships and the contract between Twin Souls.

I have woven this subject matter into the previous pages of this book, and so with that in mind, I shall share a short discourse on this particular subject matter.

I was researching today online and I came across a picture of two Egyptian beings, a husband and a wife, and the husband and the wife were both depicted as having long hair. The article went on to say that in ancient Egyptian times, men were given permission to grow their hair if they had attained a certain level of spiritual power within them to mirror the divine feminine.

This ancient truth is also depicted in the tarot, whereby the zero card is the fool, and the first card is the magician. In the first card we see that the magician holds the book of knowledge – the Torah – closed, and he has his staff reaching up into the air symbolizing that he is a receptacle of divine energy.

The second card in the tarot is the high priestess, and on this card we see that the high priestess is depicted on a throne with the book of Knowledge, the Torah, open.

This symbolizes and signifies that she has been granted graceful benevolence by our creator God to understand the book of knowledge because as the divine feminine and the carrier of the womb portal, she has been deemed less corruptible egoically than the divine masculine; therefore, in all ancient mythology and deep esoterica, including high-level masonic teachings, we discover the truth of the power of the divine feminine and how she is deeply revered in Esotericism.

Bearing that in mind, I would like to share my own individual gnosis and my own personal journey with this.

I experienced my initial spiritual awakening in the Himalayas when I was 21 years of age. And through that experience I become one with my I AM presence and my egoic identity merged into the ocean of all that is.

Through that experience, when I experienced the Satsang with God, this resulted in the birthing of my divine self – Jen the Christ.

And so, due to the auspiciousness of this experience and the fact that my divine feminine soul had contracted to experience such a profound plutonic death and rebirth in this lifetime, I quickly came to the realization that my divine masculine was still very much caught up in Maya's web and was truly identifying himself with the matrix being that his secular identity was imposing upon him.

Having liberated myself from this burden, I came to recognize that it was my duty to aid in the emergence of this aspect of my divine masculine – his eternal, childlike innocence.

This revelation clearly showed me that his role was to get us into this realm in the first place. And whilst incarnated in these vessels his role is to protect me, to protect us and to provide the physical mansion or palace that we are worthy of living in in this lifetime.

I awakened to the remembrance that his role has been ordained to be the protector and the provider.

From a spiritual perspective, my awakening showed me that my role is specifically to do with offering and harnessing great levels of protection on the spiritual planes of consciousness,

This translates as follows: Having attained unity with my avatar Christed self, I possess the ability to access and safeguard the most potent spiritual protection codes in the cosmos for both myself and my twin flame,

Consequently, I have personally experienced leading the birthing process of my own divinity. This has equipped me with the tools and wisdom to assist in the birth (through my pure spiritual womb) of the eternal Christic identity of my true heart's beloved.

What is being spoken about here is a very important and a fundamental aspect of the leadership that the feminine holds within this partnership.

I believe that this is also deeply connected primarily to the initial healing stages of any tantric union, whereby it is deeply appropriate for the divine feminine in her healed sexual priestess self, to invite her priest, the divine masculine into the chamber or the temple of divine sexual innocence, and begin the physicalization of the sexual act in order to deeply assist them personally as well as the collective to let go of all of the horrendous practices and programs that have come about due to the secularization of the sacred act of sex.

And then, once the couple has healed to a pronounced and stabilized level, I believe that the leadership role of the divine feminine is not so fixed. And the divine masculine is able, really and deeply, from an authentically healed place, to take on the role of sexual leadership, which leads to deep, deep surrender by the divine feminine towards the divine masculine.

But the divine feminine will never, ever surrender to an unhealed divine masculine. She may act as if she's surrendering, but from the perspective of her deepest inner child self, she is not surrendering. She is only able to surrender to a masculine who has absolutely purified his base level relationship with his sexuality and is able to meet her in the highest holiest sexually, innocent place.

This is a huge subject, and a huge area to discuss. And, of course, the absolute depths of these teachings cannot possibly be conveyed in this introductory manual to Lingam worship.

But what we have here is an introduction to powerful life-changing concepts – concepts and ideas that are leading us first class into the sexual revolution that we are all here to experience and anchor.

It is my deepest hope and prayer that this has opened up an avenue of fascination and excitement to go forward and embody these new sexuality codes.

I believe that women and men are leaders in different ways and at different times in their sacred union with each other. And the leadership that is spoken about is not an egoic one-upmanship leadership. It is leadership that is based in the realms of vibration, and it is never an overt leadership per se. It is a vibrational leadership reality that is being experienced.

And this leadership vibration can be likened to tuning forks – if a high-pitched tuning fork vibrates in the same space as a dull tuning fork, the dull resonant tuning fork will be lifted to align with the tuning fork of the higher frequency, and this is specifically the leadership that is being spoken about in this book – not an overt old paradigm leadership where there is third dimensional submission.

This is not a part of this experience.

It's very important that we make that clear, which in itself is another entirely deep subject matter for a whole other book.

Let us now move into the next chapter.

CHAPTER 20

HOW THE DIVINE FEMININE IS DEEPLY ENCODED IN HER SPIRITUAL BLUEPRINT TO WORSHIP THE LINGAM

In this chapter, I would like to speak about how the divine feminine is deeply encoded in her spiritual blueprint to worship the Lingam through the understanding of what it is and what it represents on a spiritual level.

In this chapter, I aim to explore the fascinating topic of our Christed sexuality blueprint. To start, I invite us to visualize the genesis story of Adam and Eve.

In this tale, Adam is depicted as being born first, followed by Eve. Both are introduced into a world of duality, where contrasts like black and white, up and down, God and the devil, good and evil abound. This narrative introduces the concept that as our two physical eyes open, our inner eye closes, leading us to perceive others as separate from ourselves. This separation fosters an identification with the material world, a part of the matrix we are all entangled within.

But yet beyond the world that occurs for us when we open our eyes, also lies the exquisite truth of the eternal union – Adam and Eve, Shiva and Shakti,

Krishna and Radharani, and Rama and Sita.

All of these divine couples / divine pairs are absolutely symbolic of the fact that our souls are created androgynously as masculine and feminine vibrational essences within one whole unified microcosm of reality.

Today, we delve into the soul contract essence of Shiva and Shakti, Krishna and Radharani. From this core, we explore the profound devotion Eve holds for her beloved Adam. It all stems from the truth that we inhabit a realm of absolute, pure, unspeakable love — a pulsating, exquisite reality. Within this love lie vast oceans of compassion, remembrance, and profound wisdom about our true essence. When the divine feminine purifies herself to merge with her vibrational counterpart, her beloved, she embodies codes of devotion and remembrance of his essence and worthiness.

And thus, we may conclude that devotion is born of wisdom. Devotion is born of eyes that are truly open and can truly see the sacredness of every breath, of every moment, in every heart that beats.

When one's eyes are open to eternal spiritual truth, the energy that rushes forward is perpetual devotion, and a deep and profound understanding that the beloved has been created for us to have an acute experience of devotion so that we may imbibe this devotional nectar back into the collective energetic web that binds all of us together in this cosmic soup of duality and oneness.

Coexisting side by side, the divine feminine has been coded to recognize the divine masculine as the innocent son of God, the Christed being that he truly is. Through the birthing of her own sacred innocence, she is thus able to see him without the filter of the third dimensional matrix programming. In her recognition and perception of him, his Christed self is born.

This is an alchemical act that is spoken about in the highest sacred esoteric literature.

An intense part of the journey of self-realization is reaching the point whereby we ultimately ascend with our highest divine sexual partner in the multiverse, which is something that those of us on the Twin flame path are vibrationally aligned with.

All of us on this path remember that we are encoded to be devoted to and work side by side with the masculine as he births his own divine innocence. We are designed to hold his hand as his sacred and eternal playmate, to frolic playfully with him in the eternal realms of ecstasy and bliss on a vibrational level.

As we step out of the secular into the sacred, we see with our inner eyes as opposed to the two eyes that see with profound irregularity, the true spiritual realms. Now our eyes are open, and we recognize the truth of service and devotion to the beloved of our soul.

CHAPTER 21

TWIN FLAMES AND SOUL CONTRACTS.

It is only appropriate that I devote some words in this sacred manual to speaking in more depth about soul contracts and Twin Flames.

The reason why it is an important and pertinent subject matter to speak about in this book is because the new earth sexuality paradigm, which has been downloaded by myself from the Akashic Records, holds that we will return to the pre-fall of Atlantis sexuality soul contracts. These hold that we are encouraged to abstain from sharing our sexual energy with anyone other than our highest sexual soul contracted partner.

My guides have revealed to me that this is the ultimate destination which our society is evolving towards. Currently, we are blazing a trail, igniting the initial embers of this spiritual truth within the collective consciousness as these words are shared and disseminated.

Therefore, the subject matter of twin flames and soul contracts must be spoken about in this book to offer a context with regard to the outcome and evolution of new earth sexual relationships.

So much of the codes and the teachings of this book

are born of this understanding – of this revolution in our collective sexuality, where we are collectively taking it out of the mundane base and beastly, and we are reinstating it back into the highest holiest, sacred realms. In those realms, we are awakened spiritually. We understand that we are eternal spiritual beings, and we make soul contracts with certain souls while sat at the feet of Mother Father God prior to our physical incarnation.

It is no secret that we experience our most extraordinary, ecstatic unions with those high-level soul ordained contracts.

Twin Flames

It's crucial to discuss Twin Flames because ancient teachings consistently highlight its significance as a deeply hidden evolutionary truth. Humanity has endured significant misguidance from overlords intent on distorting our remembrance of our true nature as spiritual beings.

The essence of this truth lies in the understanding that we are born as divine pairs, akin to Adam and Eve. In our current modern society, this is termed finding one's soulmate, which translated means finding one's twin flame. When anyone says they want to find their soulmate, really they're saying they want to find their twin flame.

It is such a deep desire for all of us to find that perfect being who is truly home for us, and that is what our sexuality has been blueprinted and created to experience.

As we evolve as a society away from secular programming with regards to our sexuality, I believe there will be a very important transitionary phase where there will be conversations along the manner of,

"I recognize that you are not my ultimate, highest spiritual partner and I'm happy for us to be together, but I absolutely am open to letting you go when your highest spiritual partner comes into your energetic field and vice versa."

I deeply believe that this is going to be a very, very important aspect of the transitioning societal ways and conversations that we will be having in our relationships as we transition out of the secular back into the sacred.

I trust you now recognize the profound relevance of Twin Flames and soul contracts to the sacred wisdom presented in this book. As I conclude this chapter on soul contracts, I believe that each of our pivotal moments in sexuality, leading to sacred and divine relationships, are agreements made before our birth and incarnation. Soulmates and others assist and guide us toward our highest spiritual relationships, – our twin soul, our vibrational counterpart.

There is so much to speak about on this subject matter onwards, we go.

CHAPTER 22

THE SPIRITUAL IMPACTS OF LOOSE SEXUALITY, POLYAMORY, POLYGAMY, AND MORE

In my humble opinion, I believe that the original sexual blueprint of Adam and Eve is eternally held and heralded as the operation Mundis to ascension.

In many high level spiritual circles polyamory is referred to as poly-agony. And again, this is another huge subject area that a whole book could be dedicated to speaking about, however I will just briefly mention my own perspective with regards to polyamory, Lingam worship, and the new Earth sexuality codes that are being shared and dispersed here.

It is my understanding that polyamory is a form of spiritual abuse to oneself as it entangles you energetically, at the saliva core level, with various multiple partners through whom you are then hooked into all of their partners and their partners, et cetera, et cetera.

If you are not ofay with techniques of sexual spiritual hygiene, then this is opening up your energetic field to all manner of challenges. Therefore, I often feel deeply that when we really, really ask what our heart wants, our heart wants love – our heart wants love with the one true beloved – our heart does not want love with multiple partners. And if it does – I would propose that this is a false matrix program that has been indoctrinated into you, because more than likely your sacred heart, does not want to share itself with anyone other than one's divine beloved.

As articulated in the Vedas and various mystical teachings of Shiva and Shakti, Yin and Yang, Krishna, and Radharani, it becomes evident that if this is indeed the spiritual blueprint we are meant to embody and experience, then engaging in multiple partnerships can only prove detrimental to us on a spiritual level.

All of this is said with absolutely no judgment. We are all having an experience as spirit in matter, and we experience everything personally.

However, I am reminded of the ancient tradition that tells us that when our souls depart this realm, our hearts are weighed against a feather. And if our heart is not as light as the white feather, then we simply are recycled back into this karmic loop simulation.

So, it's my deepest understanding that taking multiple partners is part of an agenda that we have been programmed to accept as a means of taking us away from our true divine original blueprint, which is all part of the energy of kali Yuga, which is concluding now.

We are moving into the beautiful and blissful energies of the Golden Age – Satya Yuga, and with that, we are bringing with us the paradigm of new, beautiful relationships.

CHAPTER 23

INTIMACY AVOIDANCE AND CO-DEPENDENCY, AND HOW THIS RELATES TO THE OLD PARADIGM OF RELATIONSHIPS.

In this chapter, I would like to speak about intimacy avoidance and codependency, how this relates to the old paradigm of relationships, and what we need to become consciously aware of in order to let go of these old modes of being.

Intimacy is a complex matter. Many of us are familiar with the broken down version of what intimacy is saying, which is "in to me I see". This is an excellent place to start with regards to understanding what intimacy truly is.

It is my deepest understanding that intimacy is always related to intimacy with one's self, one's holy, divine self. The path to intimacy with one's holy divine self traverses the deep, shadowy corridors of shadow work, resolution, forgiveness, and atonement. Through alchemy and transformation, one unravels the knots of their base consciousness, birthing the unrivalled glory of the crown—a product of profound and in-depth shadow work.

Therefore, it is my belief that intimacy can only be

mirrored. In other words, your beloved can only reflect and reciprocate the level of intimacy they hold within their own selves.

Suppose the beloved has not been avoiding intimacy with their own self by engaging in spiritual practices such as addressing triggers, atoning for distorted reflections, and undertaking necessary journaling, therapy, and counselling. In that case, true intimacy with another can be achieved.

It's only through this deep self-intimacy that one can authentically connect with their beloved on a profound level. And so there we have the very roots and the very foundation of what intimacy is. From these words, we can clearly establish that it is very rare in our culture to find one who is so profoundly adept at the ability to go so fearlessly and courageously into the depth of their own shadow consciousness.

Therefore, for the vast majority of the population, when they are met with uncomfortable reflections, challenges, and glitches in their romantic partnerships, this can very easily activate the energy of avoidance – avoidance of intimacy, enabling them to easily attach to a false narrative that one is too busy to be intimate with one's beloved.

Really, in these moments this is signalling a 100% breakdown of intimacy with one's self and absolutely within one's relationship.

There are many couples that absolutely normalize no intimacy in their relationships. And this is often justified through maternity and having children and the stress and impact that children have on relationships. And while there is truth in that, in a truly, truly healthy relationship, there will never ever be a breakdown or shutdown of intimacy; there will be 100% doors open to intimacy at every single moment.

So therefore, those of you who are reading these words, who are feeling triggered, who are feeling seen in this moment through encountering this powerful flow of reminders, it is important to note that if you want to heal your intimate relationships, heal your relationship with yourself, understand that your inner child is waiting for you to reparent them.

Your inner child is not waiting for your beloved to reparent them. Your inner child is not waiting for a therapist or anything outside of itself. Your inner child is very patiently waiting for you, the parent, the adult self, to come in and deeply and profoundly heal, comfort, soothe and restore its younger self.

When we face this deep spiritual work, we are then able to sit with the true, authentic, pain, suffering, and woundedness of the divine beloved who sits before us. And when we are able to hold that level of maturity and meeting, then all fear, shame, avoidance, and lack of intimacy symptoms simply wash away eternally. And this is the essence of new paradigm relationships.

There are many of you who are reading these words who know that you are not divinely mated with your highest spiritual partner, and you know that you have been experiencing great suffering in your relationships on a deep, spiritual level. And my heart goes out to you as you read these words, because it takes much bravery, especially for men, to leave those relationships and seek out relationships that are much more vibrationally aligned and spiritually beneficial.

So therefore, if you are reading these words and feeling emotional and triggered, please know that as you put this book down, my prayers are with you, that your highest spiritual partner comes forth instantly, and immediately, the moment that you let go of any old, outdated relationship that is not blissful, ecstatic and deeply nourishing and beautiful.

Know that you deserve that type of love and your higher self has that relationship aligned for you. But you have to let go of what is not serving you on a deep, authentic, spiritual level.

When we have the power to let go on this level, then we open ourselves up to relationships that are absolutely divinely blissful. And it is only really when that happens that we can experience the perfect matrimony. As quoted earlier, in the discourse on perfect matrimony, the author clearly states that those who are not mated correctly are the course of all strife on earth. And if you think about it, it makes perfect sense because the discordant energies between many couples in romantic relationships is most likely causing far greater anguish and distortion than benefit.

This is such a massively deep subject to speak about. And I'm sure if these words resonate for you, you will accept your responsibility to co-create this new paradigm of wondrous sacred sexuality whereby we all prepare and save ourselves to be with our highest spiritual mate on the earth at this time.

CHAPTER 24

HOW DO YOU KNOW IF YOU ARE WITH YOUR HIGHEST SPIRITUAL PARTNER?

As I have discussed extensively in this book, in my humble opinion we are all anchoring the new earth sexuality codes which are deeply connected to being prepared from birth to be with one's highest spiritual partner.

This subject matter energetically permeates all the pages of this book, and I'm sure many of you are wondering how you know if you are with your highest spiritual partner. Therefore, I feel it is deeply appropriate that I add this chapter into this book on Lingam worship

One of the first fundamental hallmarks of knowing you are with your highest spiritual partner is that you will never, ever look at anyone else. You will never find anyone else exciting because your spiritual appetite is satiated at an otherworldly level. Your cup will be over-spilling with desire and gratitude for your beloved so that you won't even notice a beautiful person when they walk past you, never mind enter into fantasy worlds of a potential relationship with them.

If you find yourself looking at other people and being

excited about other connections, this is a 100% sign from your higher self that you are not mated with the right person.

When you are mated with the correct person you will know you are home on all levels of your being, and you will feel eternal peace and calm. If you have ever experienced anxiety, that anxiety will be completely eradicated at the root level when you are with your God-ordained mate.

The main reason people in relationships feel anxiety is because their higher self is alerting them to the fact that they are not mated to the correct person on the spiritual level.

It is very important at this stage in our planetary evolution that we are mated with the correct soul, since, when we come together with our true divine partner, our love extends beyond the multiverse and opens up golden portals, enabling God's light to pour into the atmosphere.

This atmosphere is so devoid of this divine light that we have all contracted and made a spiritual promise to unite with our true soul partner.

This powerful portal energy is activated through the merge of our heart chakras, and is so powerful. It literally opens up wormholes in inner and outer space.

If you are not mated with the right person, there will be a sense of drudgery, mundanity and obligation. Your life will feel as if you are having to sacrifice your bliss and your needs for this person ad infinitum.

You will most likely delude yourself into believing that this is the correct way to function in relationships even though your higher self is face-palming and weeping at these immature and spiritually backward views that you are holding onto for dear life.

When you are mated with your highest spiritual partner you will experience the exponential expansion of your auric field. Even prior to walking into a space, everybody will feel the impact of you and your beloved's energetic union. When you are not mated with the right person, there will be absolutely zero connection on an auric field level, and when you are together there will be no impact which other people can perceive.

In fact, other people will look on your relationship and know deeply, intuitively and implicitly that you are not mated correctly.

When you are mated correctly to your highest divine partner, you will be so similar in many ways. In so many cases you will find that you will have similar styles, even a similar look, and you will be coded to fulfil exactly the same spiritual mission.

If you are not mated with the right person, you will

find your interests and passions are very, very different and you are very much pursuing an individualized spiritual mission path.

This is a profoundly clear and explicit sign that you are not mated with the right person.

Another sign that you are mated with your highest spiritual partner is the feelings of happiness and overflowing bliss. You will feel as if you have died and returned to the highest heavenly realms, and this feeling will stay with you forever.

You will not feel this when you are not mated with your highest spiritual partner. You will feel very bound to the earth realm and locked into the matrix, and what the Hindus refer to as the maya. There will be an experience of putting up with a lot of neglect, and this will be normalized when you are not mated with the right person.

When you are mated with your highest spiritual partner, you will never ever want to be out of their sight. You will find yourselves following one another everywhere naturally and magnetically because Innately you will remember that your spirits were originally one, and you very bravely chose to split and individuate as two souls. When you come back together on the physical realm, you will rationalize that you have been apart for long enough. Therefore, being apart for even a second is not appropriate.

Please note this is a very common feature of true

divine partnership.

When you are mated with your highest spiritual partner you will actively age regenerate.

When you are mated with the wrong person, you will experience an exponential intensification and acceleration of the ageing process like nothing on earth.

When you are mated with the right person, you will find that all your grey hairs will begin to disappear and your true divine GLORY will be ACTUALISED.

CHAPTER 25

ASCENSION AND LINGAM WORSHIP

We are now reaching the sections where the key themes of this book come together. I would hope that it has been firmly established in your consciousness that Lingam worship is deeply connected to ancient tantric practices, which were born of the sacred union of the Gods and the Goddesses as depicted so thoroughly and prolifically in the Indian temples.

These temple walls are teaching us and showing us who we are as Gods and Goddesses incarnated on this earthly plane with these extraordinarily blissful physical bodies.

These teachings deeply reiterate that our purpose in life is to awaken our sacredness and our divinity, and awaken to the privilege we have to cherish, love and adore our beloveds who are blessed to come into our lives.

This is absolutely one of the most important and fundamental aspects of our soul's purpose in this lifetime, and it's my hope that through reading these words, your heart has been deeply stirred, and old ancient memories that lay buried in the depths of your heart have had an opportunity to bubble up to the surface, reminding you of the endless depths of love and devotion that you hold within you and that you are here to share in this lifetime.

This book is a book of worship, and worship comes through love. The worship that is being spoken about here is not a blind asleep guru infatuation worship. It is worship, adoration, recognition, and deep reverence for the holiness and sacredness of the being before us. When you have eyes that are open and can clearly perceive the truth of the one who stands before you, worship is a natural and inevitable outcome.

Worship towards another is born of deep recognition, recognition in the holiness of life, recognition in the holiness of self, and recognition of the holiness of all that is.

With all of this in mind, let us now delve into the final chapters, aiming further to enrich the reprogramming process that has been set in motion by embracing the blessings conveyed through these sacred words.

There are many concepts in this book that may be new for some of the readers of this book; souls who find this book but are not so familiar with the ascension community and the understanding of DNA and the rapture, / The Event and such like.

These are subject matters that I covered extensively in my signature work, "Twin Flames and the Event" which, as I mentioned earlier, is an important accompaniment to really deeply understand the message of this book.

Bearing that in mind, I would like to talk about ascension, and how ascension is connected to the great tantric practice that we are discussing here.

The best analogy that I can find to describe the ascension process is the understanding that when we are born, we are born with our Kundalini serpents asleep at the base of our spine. The Kundalini serpents, ida and pingala, represent duality, and they represent identification with one's egoic construct on our spiritual path.

For those of us on the ascension path, more than likely we will have made a soul contract to trigger and awaken those kundalini serpents to come out of their dormant asleep state into their awakened erect state. In that moment when that happens, the two masculine and feminine serpents rush together, activating the ascension of the Kundalini serpents from the base chakra throughout all the chakra systems.

This is something that I experienced, and it was a very, very intense experience. And although it brought a great deal of ecstasy and bliss, it also bought with it the most gruelling physical challenges and emotional depths that I had to go through in order to integrate the light that I had encountered on top of the mountain.

This is one way to describe the ascension process, and that is – the awakening of one's kundalini energy.

A great analogy to explain the ascension process is that when we are incarnated, we are born into a society that does not recognize the divine being we are. Everyone is conditioned to identify with the outer egoic shell and believes themselves to be separate isolated islands. This can be termed caterpillar consciousness, which is the mainstream norm consciousness, also known and referred to as third-dimensional consciousness.

However, some caterpillars sign up to go through the fire of transformation, and they enter into a liquid goo and every single aspect of the caterpillar, apart from a few fundamental parts, completely breaks down, dies, and dissolves in a liquid goo. And what is born out of the chrysalis is the fabulous, beautiful butterfly. This butterfly is absolutely herself. She's free to fly wherever she wishes, she doesn't need anyone or anything. She's in ecstasy with her godly self.

This butterfly consciousness can be understood as fifth-dimensional consciousness, the consciousness of absolute moksha, absolute liberation, absolute in the present moment-ness, absolute joy of being and simply being free.

So, the ascension process is what we all go through, whether it's in this lifetime or in other lifetimes to come. We are all involved in this process of transforming, from caterpillar to butterfly.

Therefore, if we are engaging in non-sacred sexuality or entangling ourselves in low vibrational trauma-bonded karmic relationships, this can cause a huge and monumental deficit to our spiritual evolutionary trajectory.

And this process could be likened to a moment in cosmic time where the record gets scratched and the record is not able to move forward on its evolutionary path. It just keeps going round and round and round and round.

This is a karmic trap for the soul consciousness. Within these karmic traps lies an illusion of comfort, of stability, yet it is all rooted in fear. And so therefore, if one allows and tolerates these low vibrational trauma-bonded non-sacred sexual connections to continue, this massively halts and holds up your ascension process.

And again, no one is judging anyone. There is no external God judging anyone or anything. This is between you and your God self. But you have been drawn to these words for a reason. You need to understand precisely what is happening. If you are not in ecstatic bliss, if you look at other people, if you do not wake up and jump out of bed at the crack of dawn and bow in ecstasy and grace to your beloved, she's not the one. He's not the one.

We are all here to experience the most intense and potent true love that we can experience. But to do that, we have to let go of these fear-based entanglements that keep our planet locked into a nightmare third-dimensional grid patterning.

As we spoke about before, the reason why, in times gone past, we have been able to live in a crystalline higher dimensional consciousness is because these true love bonds were revered and held in the highest esteem within the highest echelons of society.

Therefore, if one is experiencing these low-grade toxic entanglements, we need to understand the vast detriment energetically that this is pumping into the collective grid, sending out deep waves of incoherence, incompatibility, and all that goes against the flow.

The ascension process is what we are all here to experience, whether we are awakened to that or not, whether we have deluded ourselves and surrounded ourselves with teachers who are keeping us locked into the third-dimensional matrix, identification, prison, whatever is going on.

These words are coming forth from the heart-core of existence to remind you of the spiritual responsibility that you have to love yourself and call into your reality and experience your highest true love relationship. You have to set boundaries within all your relationships that if they are not at this level, then you must be open to letting your partner go when that higher spiritual partner steps onto the scene.

All of this is connected to the new earth sexuality template. If you are happy and energized and have stopped the ageing process and never ever look at another person, then most likely, you are mated with your highest spiritual partner. And if that is so, then this chapter was not for you. This chapter is for those people that have deluded themselves into identifying with a fear-based thought grid, which has not only kept them in a depressive prison but is also keeping humanity's consciousness locked into this prison.

It is important that we understand about the ascension process in a conscious way when working with the teachings and principles of this book. This book is saturated in the vibrational codes of spiritual remembrance that bring forth almost in a knee-jerk reaction the energy of worship and devotion.

Worship and devotion is born of recognition. Recognition is born when we allow the old caterpillar self to die so that we may become our free, liberated, angelic human self. And that is the ascension process, becoming one with our higher self. And when we become one with our higher self, we are as children and we are humble and we are ever, ever growing to become more and more and more and more at one with our Godself.

And as we are one with our God-self, we recognize the Christed being in our brother and sister who stands before us, and that naturally evokes deep reverence and the desire to serve.

This is an energy that spills out into all areas of our life, and in this sacred manual, we have come together to speak specifically about worshiping the Lingam and the dedication of the beloved to deeply standing in reverence and abiding love towards the sacred Lingam.

Let us move on to the next chapter.

CHAPTER 26

THE DARK SIDE OF THE PHALLUS

This book would not be complete unless I paid homage to the dark side of the phallus, and offered an opportunity for all of us reading these words to alleviate the collective suffering that has been perpetuated in the name of the phallus. I would like to start this chapter by sharing with you all the vision that I had, as I was writing the concluding paragraphs to this book.

As I was going to sleep last night, having written the last chapter of this book, I had a very clear image of a little girl saying to her father sitting opposite her, "I don't like the way you said this, and I don't like the way you did that."

This opened my consciousness to a whole area of life on earth, which has witnessed the divine Masculine abusing his physically dominant power.

As I was going to sleep last night, I was receiving very powerful visions about the fact that because the divine masculine does not have a womb portal and has not been coded to be the primary nurturer to children and infants, this has created a separation codex within the masculine psyche, which enables him to detach from his humanity with far greater ease than the divine feminine.

This ability of the divine masculine to dettach from his humanity has led to all manner of despicable atrocities that we have in our world today, including sex abuse, child abuse, sex trafficking, rape, kidnapping, et cetera.

Research shows that well over 99% of these atrocities towards humanity are committed by men, and in this sacred manual on divine masculinity, it is very appropriate that we add this chapter to this book, otherwise this would not be a holistic and authentic offering.

This would simply be an agenda to portray the divine masculine with regardsKinda feel like I'm done to one aspect of his being, which is his divine aspect. On the other hand, it is clear from the history of war shed on this earth that the masculine soul has also been hugely responsible for the abuse and trauma that has been inflicted on many innocent children and women in the name of masculine domination.

I have often wondered why this occurs because women give birth to men, and the mother is the primary soul in the young boy's life. I concur that something must occur in that moment of raising that child whereby the child sees that the divine feminine is disrespected and dishonoured, and therefore he takes it upon himself to perpetuate the pattern of causing suffering towards the divine feminine.

What is the remedy to this situation?

The remedy, I believe, lies with women and mothers, finding their strict boundaries, particularly with their sons, training their sons to be the devotional pillars that they have incarnated to be, training their sons to be the material providers and protectors for the divine feminine and giving sons a profoundly important spiritual perspective and purpose in their life.

I believe that this is the antidote to all war suffering and abuse at the hands of the divine masculine.

I believe that when we live in a society whereby we are all mated with our highest spiritual partner, all children will grow up in an environment where they will absorb the true love codes. These true love codes hold the vibration of deep respect, deep honour and deep reverence, particularly towards the mother.

As the divine masculine grows up in this environment, this programme will naturally slip into his software operating system and he will absolutely emulate this respect and reverence in his relationships when he leaves his childhood home.

We must address this issue and bring great healing and comfort to the divine masculine soul who wishes to celebrate separation and cause pain and suffering.

There is a tribe in Africa in which, if one of the souls acts out of line or is abusive to another person in the tribe, that person is placed in the centre and all of the tribe members sing the song that came through in the moment of that child's birth. This is because every child is assigned a song or a melody, which must be sung to them if they ever forget who they are and their spiritual path.

On top of that, every member of the tribe tells them all the things that they love about them and all the deep things that they appreciate about them. This has been proved to recorrect the nefarious acting out and cause an alignment back with a highly beautiful way of being – for that particular person.

I believe that we must create the village again in our society. It takes a village to raise a child, and it takes a village to prepare humanity, to be the empathic, compassionate, intelligent beings that we are all coded to be. Modern society has sought to create separation, particularly in the living styles that we inhabit. Take for example, where I live. I live in a beautiful, detached house on a road full of other beautiful, detached houses, but there is no community.

There is no coming together of the community.

None of the neighbours seem to know each other, and that is the way the old controllers have wanted it to be.

Keeping humanity cut off and separate from each other engenders the belief of threat. We must address this issue now if we are really going to step into our devotional codons and start earthing the new Earth sexuality codes.

It is absolutely fundamentally important that we address this glitch in the masculine psyche that enables him to cut off and switch off empathically from the suffering of others.

This needs to be corrected and brought into balance if we are truly going to ground this new earth way of being.

CHAPTER 27

CONCLUSION – BOUNDARIES AND PRACTICES ON HOW TO WORK WITH THE TEACHINGS OF THIS BOOK.

By now, hopefully, your erotic juices will be flowing. Your heart will be having heart orgasms left, right and centre, and your crown chakra will be absolutely buzzing.

I would assume that is what is happening for many of you at this stage in the great journey that we have all been on.

So, to conclude, I would like to bring together everything that we have discussed and talk about practices and ways to work with the teachings of this book.

What a journey this has been, mainly for myself, having to go into the deepest depth of sexual shame to meet the energy of Shiva in that place. And through the embodied meeting with Shiva, understanding exactly what the phallus is, and in that moment of understanding what the phallus is, falling to my knees in deep, deep devotion towards my divine masculine brother for all that he has endured on a spiritual level to be incarnated in the physical plane at this time.

I never would've imagined I would birth this book at this stage in my life, but the twists and turns of life are amazing, and some things are just meant to be.

Hopefully, we are all holding this powerful ancient reminder in the forefront of our hearts now, but how do we go forward in the world as carriers of this ancient truth?

I absolutely believe that the highest path is authenticity and transparency: showing up in your reality, truly and absolutely as who you are.

And along with that, setting very, very vigilant boundaries around the level of love, friendship, and sexual love that you will allow into your energetic space.

The concept of sacred boundaries is vast and profound. In fact, I dedicated my second book, entitled "No More Crumbs," to delving deeply into the extraordinary importance and transformative potential of establishing and maintaining firm spiritual boundaries across all aspects of our lives.

I do highly recommend reading that book. If you have enjoyed this journey that we have been on so far in, in "No More Crumbs," I share an extraordinarily powerful technique called The Red Circle Technique. Many thousands of people have learned this technique and used it to bring about extraordinarily swift transformation.

It is an ascension code, a transformational

consciousness tool that speaks directly to the subconscious mind, informing it to take very direct and serious action.

Please see my accompanying workbook whereby I will share the link to the Red Circle meditation.

Within these pages, it is paramount to stress the importance of boundaries because they are deeply intertwined with your vibrational experience. Your vibrational state consistently mirrors the boundaries you maintain, and as you advance on your spiritual journey, the reflections that prompt you become more immediate, revealing where your boundaries are either firm or loose.

Boundaries are an act of constant refinement.

And as spiritual warriors, we must always be vigilant, aware of and appreciative of the reflections we receive on the external that show us that we need to upgrade our boundaries in this particular incident.

The more we show that we love ourselves and the more we say no to people, relationship situations and situationships that are not loving, the quicker we let go of all of the heavy, energetic crust that has been keeping us tethered to the lower dimensions and stuck in the world of caterpillars.

This is all part of the spiritual evolutionary process to which Lingam worship is deeply connected.

Perhaps upon seeing the title of this book, you may

have assumed it was a sex manual. However, as you've journeyed through its pages, it becomes evident that it is a profound exploration of spiritual remembrance—a conquest that resonates deeply with all of us.

Our hearts have been deeply aroused and excited to receive this most important information from the ancient realms – that we are the harbingers of the new sexuality codes.

And we now stand as the army of light warriors who say no to all sexual meetings that are not of the highest, most beautiful, purest love.

And we recognize the holiness of sexual merging and approach it in a reverent and sacred way.

Each of us is burning a sacred sexuality flame and we are collectively burning a sacred sexuality flame. And it starts with us. And like wildfire, it rapidly catches because this is every single soul's original divine blueprint.

We are one energy of God that has fractalled into billions of personalities and aspects.

Our core blueprint is 100% identical.

We are all encoded to be fully actualized and to recognize the holiness of existence of ourselves and of all of our brothers and sisters.

And indeed, this is exactly what our journey together has been all about. So, how do we work with the teachings of this book?

We deepen our spiritual practice. We deepen our sadhana. We get up at dawn, we take exercise, we cut out sugar, we cut out all mucus-forming foods and we deeply take care of our body. We meditate, we play music. We follow our bliss. We read. We constantly want to learn and keep expanding our knowledge. We spend time in nature. We follow our passion, follow our bliss. We keep traveling. We live in abundant consciousness. We say yes to our most extraordinarily high level existence, We stand committed to being able to say no when necessary, and we stay humble, knowing that however far we believe we have reached, we all stand as children at the feet of our creator, mother, father, God.

We hold steadfast to the knowledge that our awareness is constantly expanding and evolving.

So, we work with this information through bettering, polishing, and fortifying our innermost being.

We are all being fortified just as steel fortifies. And it is my most profound prayer that we all run towards the fortification process. We run into the darkness; we run into the shadow, bringing the greatest light of our childlike, playful divine, eternal, holy self – fearlessly meeting all dragons, monsters and shadows. We meet it all with grace, love, a smile, happiness and a song.

And all the monsters become our friends. And that is

how we live the teachings of this book.

We become one with our higher self. We become the genuine spiritual master that we were born to be.

We commit to our spiritual practice. We commit to going on rampages of gratitude.

We commit to being the observer of the monkey mind and being deeply committed to present moment consciousness.

We commit to doing deep meditations and working with pure and aligned mentors to assist us and so much more.

I would like to speak a few words about what happens in our life when we practice Lingam worship as a man and as a woman.

As a man, if you practice Lingam worship, this is how it would look. You are at one with the teachings of this book. You understand that you have been through a lot on a spiritual level, and you deserve to be held by your queen, your one and only queen who loves you unconditionally and who loves every single battle scar that you hold, who will lovingly kiss and caress every single battle scar that you hold.

She will kiss every single part of you. She's not the frog, she's not the fake one. She's the real one. She's your eternal queen. And it is my understanding that through reading this book, your faith will be 100% restored and a commitment will be activated in your field to let go of all lower vibrational hookups, connections, et cetera, et cetera.

And from now on you will only be available for your highest spiritual queen in the universe. And when she comes into your life, most likely she will have read this book. And if she hasn't read this book, you can share this book with her and explain the impact that it has had on your life receiving these reminders from ancient times.

And if she really truly is your queen, she will be vibrationally aligned with you and these teachings. And most likely she will weep very, very deep tears when she receives this sacred reminder. And together, you will absolutely embark on the journey of the highest sacred sexual path. And of course, it must be stressed that sex with our highest spiritual partner is everything. But at its deepest core, it is playful and innocent, and it is natural, and it is the most natural form of expression in the creation. And therefore, it will include such a level of comfort and oneness that every element of one's being will be fulfilled in that sexual connection.

And within that, there will be a reverence. There will be a ceremony, there will be dates, there will be intentions and times where you will come together as if you were going to the temple and you literally come to the temple of your beloved, and you bring your offerings, and you make puja, and you do your Abhishek – your milk and honey cleanse. And this is all part of reverence towards the divine, which is what keeps the holy fires burning and pumping out, keeping this world lit with the true vibration of God. The reason why we're all here is that we're all here to be one with our God self and be in the ecstatic flow and vibration of our God self.

And therefore, all of these teachings are connected to that one primary purpose. So, if you are a man reading these words, you will align with a beloved who is ready to go on this journey with you. And you will bow deeply to her yoni and she will bow deeply to your Lingam and you will recognize it as the holy temple that it is.

And if you are a woman reading these words, please apply the same boundaries of not accepting anyone into your energetic field unless it is a high spiritual soul contract. Then from that place you will start embarking on the path of tantra and sacred sexuality, having a conversation about semen retention, understanding that the semen is truly the life force of the masculine and the squandering of it is deeply connected to high levels of anger depletion and low energy and serves to deplete the christos oil that the divine masculine holds, which is part of his longevity blueprint.

And I would hold out for your king, your beloved spiritual consort, and when he comes into your life, most likely he would have read this book and you will both stand and recognize each other and commit to the path of sacred sexuality.

I very much look forward to bringing through the yoni worship book, and I very much look forward to bringing through the accompanying workbook that goes with this book.

I do hope that you get a chance to look at the appendix and the bibliographies, and I really hope that you come and join all of my platforms and find me on social media where I'm very active.

Please let me know how this book was for you.

I'm truly open to receive all your messages and emails in love and eternal light.

Jen.

AFTERWORD

WHY DO WE OFFER LINGAM WORSHIP?

In this chapter, I would like to speak about the implications when we approach the lingam with honour, worship, and reverence for the masculine, the feminine, and the collective consciousness of humanity.

We have all been born into a society that has absolutely denied and neglected our true spiritual essence. There has been an insidious agenda that has sought to capitalize on humanity's base nature, with an ensuing hijacked programming agenda; creating it such that humanity, particularly in the West, has completely forgotten about its holy, divine origins.

This has had huge implications for us as a society and has had huge implications for us individually.

For men, the implications of this have been desperately detrimental. In our society, the sacred Masculine has been conditioned to associate with his egoic self and to believe that he should impulsively pursue any lustful desire arising from his lower chakras.

When a divine, holy, blueprinted man acts out in this detrimental, unconscious way, this causes disease on the energetic plane of consciousness; This disease can manifest as glitches, knots, shadows and black holes in the auric field.

These issues then manifest in the man's life with further addiction to the pursuit of lower-chakra base activities and a further descent into the forgetfulness of his true spiritual origins.

Therefore, when we as an awakened feminine and awakened partner recognize the divine Masculine for who he truly is as God's innocent son, and we recognize what the holy phallus member symbolizes and represents, and thus approach the phallus with that recognition and inevitable reverence, this attitude absolutely has the capacity to shake and awaken the divine masculine out of his programmed comatose state and perpetual identification with his third-dimensional dualistic identity.

When we approach the phallus with recognition and reverence, this plants the seed for the new Earth sexuality codes. And just like a lemon tree or an apple tree, these seeds will grow into vast trees, which will create vast forests and will be so huge that our descendants will be able to seek shelter under their branches.

When we approach the divine phallus member with recognition and reverence, we trigger the activation of his Christed blueprint that has laid dormant in his unconscious field, and it will ultimately come back online, bringing with it downloads for his consciousness that will saturate his being with the remembrance of who he truly is as God's eternal, holy and innocent son.

When these energies are experienced by the divine masculine, this is the crowning of the divine Masculine's soul blueprint, and he is then able to take out the crown which has been waiting patiently in his etheric field and place that crown directly on his own head, because ultimately, this is a sovereign universe, which means that we must all Crown our own selves.

That is how this universe operates. When the divine masculine places the crown on his holy head, this is symbolic of the actualization of his Christed self.

When the divine masculine expresses in this plane of consciousness from the level of his Christed self, he becomes:
A powerful, magnetic leader of hearts,
A leader of men,
A leader of women.
He becomes a teacher in the true spiritual sense,

And his magic, charisma, magnetism, and sublime nature will be experienced consciously or unconsciously by every single soul who is blessed to encounter him.

This will also mark the ending of the reincarnation cycle of that particular soul strand, and it will fully ascend back to the Godhead as full mastery will have been achieved.

It is important to note that many souls who complete their evolutionary timeline choose to return to the lower dimensional planes of consciousness to serve and be volunteers particularly in universes which are experiencing transformation and spiritual shifts.

The healing that is available for the divine feminine who practices Lingam worship are:

She is able to fully become one with her eternal priestess self, the one who has practised the ways of sacred sexuality and mastering Kundalini tantric energy in many dimensional realities and other universes.

The divine feminine is able to experience the fullness of her unconditional God heart, which loves the divine Masculine so deeply.

There are no words that could adequately depict how deeply the divine feminine loves the divine Masculine.

Imagine thousands upon thousands of oceans of depth. This is the way to explain the depth of love the divine feminine feels towards the masculine.

Therefore, when she is familiarized with these powerful tantric teachings and reminders, she is able to become one with her divine priestess self. And this brings oceanic depth of healing, recalibration and coherence into her entire system.

She knows that she's serving her higher self in the recognition of her divine masculine. She knows that she's serving God in her recognition of the divine masculine's holy self,

And she knows that she's serving her divine Masculine on the deepest level of his soul, And she knows that she promised her divine Masculine that she would recognize him and be devoted to him in this manner. There are so many huge benefits that come from Lingam worship practice. Through this divine practise the divine feminine is also planting powerful seeds that are birthing the new earth. These are new earth sexuality seeds which will grow into trees and forests, under whose shade our future descendants will rest.

The divine feminine who comes to this practice becomes a trailblazer, a ways-shower, a leader in consciousness, and she ultimately becomes one with her higher self.

This brings deep wisdom, happiness, bliss, downloads, awakening, enlightenment, remembrance, psychic powers, spiritual powers, manifestational powers, charisma, magnetism, all of it.

All of this is born from this practice. As a society that practices Lingam worship, the benefits are:

We will slowly, in a drip, drip fashion, begin to see the implications of this divine practice being taken on by members in our society.

When we as a society awaken to this ancient knowledge and truth, we will build temples and spaces in honour and reverence of this, just like the temples that were built in ancient India.

We will completely curate our whole societal system to facilitate, hold space for, enhance and deepen this vibrational truth. We will end the nefarious programming attack on humanity, which took place at the time of the fall of Atlantis.

This hijacking will be absolutely severed at its core, which I actually believe it truly, truly is now. And as I write these words in March 2024, I believe that very, very rapidly, we will see the birthing of these sacred societies that are being spoken about.

We will have a school system which will recognize the holiness and divinity of each child.

We will have a hospital service which will recognize the power of frequency, colour and sound, a hospital service which will completely eradicate invasive surgical procedures and truly work with God's greatest healing modality, which is frequency, sound and colour.

We will have media that are filled with beautiful, exquisite, spiritually enhancing information, which will be pouring through all the channels

We will live in a society that is created with stunningly beautiful architecture like the Sistine Chapel, like some parts of the Vatican, like the tartarian buildings such as St. Paul's cathedral, and the Hindu temples.

All of these structures were created with the devotion, which is being spoken about in this book. As a society, we will progress towards this state of spiritual maturity. We will come full cycle with our old ancient ancestors who created those monumental architectural structures which would last forever.

I have decided to add this chapter as the afterward of the book, I am currently in the process of editing the workbook that accompanies this book. I would like to take this opportunity to remind everyone who reads this book that I would highly recommend working with the accompanying workbook, as I give you many practical techniques, teachings and direct instruction with regards to how to apply Lingam worship practices into your life.

I've poured an equal amount of love and wisdom into the creation of the workbook as I have into this book.

All that being said, I am signing off now and I'm deeply looking forward to hearing from you all, sharing with me your experiences of receiving this book, reading this book, and becoming one with the teachings of this book.

Please feel free to email me at cosmicgypsy33@gmail.com.

I'll be happy to receive your emails.

In love and eternal light, Jen.

APPENDIX

In Hinduism, the ritual of abhishekam (also spelled as "abhisheka" or "abishek") involves the pouring or bathing of a deity's idol or lingam (symbol of the divine) with various sacred substances, including milk and honey, among others.

During an abhishekam ceremony, devotees perform a series of rituals to honour and worship the deity. The pouring of milk and honey over the idol or lingam is believed to purify and energize the divine presence, while also symbolizing offerings of abundance, nourishment, and sweetness to the deity.

Milk is considered highly auspicious in Hindu rituals, symbolizing purity, fertility, and the essence of life. It is often offered to deities as a form of worship and devotion. Similarly, honey holds symbolic significance, representing sweetness, healing, and spiritual nourishment.

The combination of milk and honey in abhishekam highlights the devotee's desire for the divine blessings of abundance, prosperity, and spiritual fulfilment. It is believed that participating in such rituals with sincerity and devotion brings divine grace and blessings to the devotees.

Overall, the use of milk and honey in Hindu abhishekam ceremonies reflects the deep symbolism and spiritual significance attributed to these sacred substances in the worship of the divine.

Semen retention from a Vedic perspective

From a Vedic perspective, semen retention, known as "Brahmacharya," holds significant spiritual and health benefits. In Vedic philosophy, semen is considered a vital energy source known as "ojas" or "vital fluid."

Here are some benefits of semen retention from a Vedic viewpoint:

Conservation of Vital Energy: Semen is believed to contain a concentrated form of life force energy. By conserving semen through retention, individuals can harness this energy to nourish the body, mind, and spirit.

Enhanced Physical and Mental Strength: Vedic texts suggest that retaining semen strengthens the body and mind, promoting physical vitality and mental clarity. It is believed to enhance endurance, concentration, and overall well-being.

Spiritual Awakening: Practicing semen retention is viewed as a means of spiritual cultivation. By conserving and transmuting sexual energy, individuals can elevate their consciousness, deepen their spiritual practice, and attain higher states of awareness.

Increased Spiritual Awareness: Semen is considered a potent substance that, when conserved, can be sublimated into higher forms of spiritual energy. This heightened spiritual awareness enables individuals to experience greater inner peace, wisdom, and spiritual insight.

Balanced Emotions and Relationships: Semen retention encourages individuals to develop greater self-control and emotional balance. By channelling sexual energy creatively and consciously, practitioners can cultivate harmonious relationships and avoid the pitfalls of impulsive behaviour.

Overall, from a Vedic perspective, semen retention is revered as a powerful practice for physical health, mental clarity, spiritual evolution, and harmonious living. It is seen as a sacred discipline that empowers individuals to tap into their innate potential and align with the divine essence within.

Delving deeper into the Vedic perspective on semen retention reveals profound insights into its benefits:

Sublimation of Energy: In Vedic philosophy, sexual energy (or "kundalini") is considered one of the most potent forms of energy within the human body. Through semen retention, this energy is conserved and redirected upwards along the spine, facilitating the awakening of the dormant spiritual potential at the base of the spine (the "Muladhara chakra"). This process, known as "kundalini awakening," is believed to lead to spiritual enlightenment and self-realization.

Enhanced Vitality and Longevity: According to

Ayurveda, the traditional system of medicine in India closely linked with Vedic teachings, semen is considered a vital essence ("ojas") that nourishes the body and mind. By practicing semen retention, individuals preserve and replenish this vital essence, resulting in increased physical strength, resilience, and longevity.

Purification of Body and Mind: In the Vedic tradition, sexual energy is closely associated with desire and attachment, which are considered obstacles to spiritual growth. By abstaining from ejaculation and sublimating sexual energy through practices such as meditation, yoga, and self-reflection, individuals purify their minds and free themselves from the grip of worldly desires. This purification process fosters inner peace, mental clarity, and emotional balance.

Harmonization of Relationships: Semen retention encourages individuals to cultivate deeper and more meaningful relationships based on mutual respect, understanding, and spiritual connection rather than solely physical gratification. By conserving and channelling sexual energy consciously, practitioners foster intimacy, emotional intimacy, and spiritual communion with their partners, leading to greater harmony and fulfilment in relationships.

Alignment with Cosmic Rhythms: According to Vedic teachings, the human body is a microcosm of the universe, and its rhythms are intricately connected with those of the cosmos. Semen retention aligns individuals with the natural cycles of creation and preservation, allowing them to attune to the divine order of the universe and experience a sense of unity with all of creation.

In summary, from a Vedic perspective, semen retention is not merely a physical practice but a holistic approach to health, well-being, and spiritual evolution. It encompasses the integration of body, mind, and spirit and facilitates the journey towards self-realization and union with the divine.

Hindu history on Lingam worship

Hindu history provides a rich and nuanced perspective on lingam worship, which is deeply rooted in ancient traditions and spiritual beliefs. The lingam, often associated with Lord Shiva, symbolizes the creative energy of the universe and the masculine aspect of divinity. The worship of the lingam is believed to date back thousands of years, with references found in the Vedas, the oldest sacred texts of Hinduism.

The lingam is typically depicted as a cylindrical stone or pillar, representing the cosmic pillar or axis around which the universe revolves. It is revered as a manifestation of Shiva's power and is worshipped with profound devotion and reverence. Devotees believe that by worshipping the lingam, they can attain spiritual enlightenment, liberation, and divine blessings.

Throughout Hindu history, various temples dedicated to Shiva and his lingam have been constructed across the Indian subcontinent. These temples serve as sacred sites for devotees to offer prayers, perform rituals, and seek spiritual guidance. The rituals associated with lingam worship often involve offerings of water, milk, honey, and flowers, symbolizing purification, nourishment, and devotion.

Lingam worship is not merely a religious practice but also holds deep philosophical significance within Hinduism. It represents the union of the masculine and feminine energies, symbolizing the inseparable connection between Shiva and his consort, Shakti, the divine feminine. The lingam is seen as the source of all creation and the ultimate reality beyond form and attributes.

Over the centuries, lingam worship has evolved and diversified, with different regions and communities incorporating their unique customs and rituals. Despite these variations, the core essence of reverence and devotion towards the lingam remains central to Hindu spirituality, continuing to inspire and uplift millions of devotees worldwide.

How to work with the Christ oil

This is from the great teachings of Santos Banocci

Please see my accompanying workbook that goes with this book whereby I share a meditation that will directly guide you on how to connect with the Christ oil within you.

Do you know about alchemical sexual alchemy? There are 33 vertebrae in your spine. There were 33 years in the life of Jesus.

This substance comes from your medulla, makes the trip down your spine to your sacrum, which is Christ coming down into human form. And if you don't squander that essence, that sexual essence, it ascends again and goes back up to heaven, which is your thing. It's also the story of Santa Claus. Why he comes down the chimney is because this juice or this whatever substance actually passes what's called the claustrum, which is where they got Santa Claus. So, it goes down the chimney and back up the chimney.

The brain contains the cerebrum, the claustrum sits right there in the middle of the head, virtually. The claustrum secretes brain fluid. And this fluid is an oil. In ancient times, this fluid was called in Greek called christos, or the Christ. It's this beautiful fluid which comes from the cerebrum and pours down the spinal cord. It goes down the spinal cord and it reaches the sacral plexus, right next door to the sacrum, which are the five second bottom-most fused vertebrae bones at the bottom of the spinal column. The bottom-most portion of the spinal column is called the coccyx. Then just above that is the sacrum, five fused bones.

The sacral plexus is connected to the sacrum, and the fluid which comes from the cerebrum pours down the spinal cord and comes to this, the bottom-most part of the spinal cord. The claustrum is otherwise known as the holy claustrum, simply because of this beautiful oil, this christos that it secretes. You see, the word secret comes from secretion, because this secretion is a secret, and the sacrum is the sacred part of the secret. The secretion pours down the spinal cord and reaches the sacrum in the marvellous way in which our body has been designed.

The spinal cord is basically just an extension of the brain because it also does thinking. You see, the holy claustrum is otherwise known as the Santa Claustrum because this fluid that goes down to the sacred plexus is a sacred fluid. This is where the story of Santa Claus bringing presents down the chimney comes from. It's a story of physiology, and the Bible is a beautiful manual of physiological regeneration. What happens with this fluid is that every month when the moon is in the sign where your sun was when you were born, a germ or a seed is planted in the solar plexus, which is just above the sacral plexus.

And that germ is the oil, the Christ, which is born in Bethlehem. Because the solar plexus is otherwise known as Bethlehem, where the seed or the Christ is born. That seed, that oil, needs to return whence it came in the midbrain. You see, as the oil ascends the spinal cord, the vibration of the oil of the Christ increases. And the oil is first differentiated in the pineal gland and the pituitary gland before it is sent down the spinal cord. The pineal gland is the electric portion and the pituitary gland is the magnetic portion.

After the oil is differentiated it is brought down the spinal cord via the pingala and the ida nerves. These are otherwise known as the kundalini and the kundabuffer. The oil arrives at the sacral plexus and awaits the germinating of the seed once a month, twelve times a year. If we are able to transmute that seed and cause it to rise, as it rises in the spinal cord it eventually reaches the medulla oblongata, the pons and the midbrain. It crosses the vagus nerve, otherwise known as the pneumogastric nerve.

This is a nerve which descends from the brain area, from the pineal and pituitary glands respectively, and it feeds the lungs and the stomach. It's a network of nerves, and this network of nerves is called the tree of life. The ancients knew that this seed that is born in Bethlehem once a month is the Christ, and that if one were to abstain from sex during that period, that oil and seed would be saved. It would rise and it would burst through the heart chakra, through the throat chakra, and eventually the oil would arrive with its higher vibration, because at the bottom the oil has a very low vibratory rate. On the other hand, with proper practices, meditation, breathing, good eating and good peaceful behaviour, one is able to raise that Christ, that oil, so that it crosses the vagus nerve at the top of the 33 vertebrae spinal column.

This is because the Christ was crucified at 33 years of

age. When the oil arrives at the very, very top, the optic thalamus, an egg-shaped organ in the middle of the head, awaits it. When it crosses this pneumogastric nerve this is called the crucifixion. The oil is not killed and destroyed, but it is magnified 1000-fold. The oil then touches the optic thalamus, and for two and a half days remains in a condition that is considered to be dead, before reaching the pineal gland and illuminating the optic thalamus and the pineal gland. The optic thalamus was known as the light of the world by the Egyptians and the Greeks because they knew their physiology and anatomy. They knew that this precious oil which descended from the claustrum in the cerebrum was differentiated in the pineal and pituitary glands and descended the spinal cord.

They knew that it would ascend eventually and that the enlightened portion of mankind would be able to cause this Christ oil to ascend so that it would ascend to the optic thalamus and cause it to be illuminated. What in turn happens is that millions of brain cells that were dormant are now awakened. This means that there are practices which are very, very detrimental to this oil. Examples are overeating and alcohol, and sex practised at the wrong time. These practices destroy the seed and are known as eating from the tree of life because the ancients knew that once the oil is depleted because of riotous living, the fleshly organism dies.

Death results from using up all of the oil. The oil that

descends from the cerebrum is otherwise known as the manna from heaven. Heaven means heaved up, and the head, the cranium, the dome which sits on top of the torso, was known as the heavens. The heart area and the heart chakra was known as the midgard, or the middle garden. The generative area was known as Sodom and Gomorrah, the area of animal desire, and otherwise known as Egypt, hell and the world, whereas the Garden of Eden and the land flowing with milk and honey, is upstairs. In fact, the pineal gland produces a secretion known as honey, which contains DMT, and the pituitary body secretes the milk. This is the milk and honey, so that the land flowing with milk and honey is upstairs.

This is a sacred secret, simply because the secretion, which comes from the sacral plexus, is one of the most important things that we need to know for physiological regeneration. By saving the seed, one can actually live longer. In fact, the ancients used to live for thousands of years by protecting and keeping this secret and guarding it. The Egyptians built ascension chambers or pyramids for this very purpose, and they taught the science of respecting, keeping, guarding and looking after this beautiful oil. If you know the gospels well, you will know all the scriptures that refer to it.

Jesus said, "I am the light of the world. He that follows me shall not walk in darkness." The light of the world is the optic thalamus. "Keep your eye simple for if your eye is dark, your whole body will be dark." The pineal gland has always been known as the third eye. In fact, it's the spiritual eye. Most churchgoers will be denying this because in their minds Jesus Christ is a historical person who must return physically in order to save them because they cannot save themselves. They need a vicarious third party saviour, whereas the opposite is true.

This is what the so-called Apostle Paul was talking about when he referred to the sacred secret of the Christ within, the Christ that dwelleth within. For you see, the kingdom of God is within, it's not without. And in fact, the words of Jesus are pretty clear where it says, "Do not be looking out there, for the kingdom of God will not come with striking observableness." Don't look here and don't look there because there will be deceivers saying, "Oh, there he is, here is the Christ, there is the Christ." The process is within, and one must be able to raise that energy and get out of the bottom chakras. The bottom chakras deal with sexuality, strife, envy, power, greed, wealth, and all of those things.

If one is constantly seeking those things and constantly eating of the fruit of the tree of life, those beautiful nerves, the pneumogastric nerve system which is responsible for bringing the oil back up, will not bring those beautiful spiritual presents. We are the ones who are responsible for channelling that oil, that Christ seed within, so that it eventually is crucified in the middle of the head. The cerebrum is hollowed out, and the midbrain and limbic system at the top of the spinal cord is the holy of holies. The cerebellum, which sits at the back of the brain, is otherwise known as the small brain.

The cerebrum is associated with the top of the head, Aries, and the cerebellum is associated with Taurus and the left brain, the male left brain. The right brain is the feminine and it is connected to the cerebrum, Aries, the God brain. The God man is the cerebrum and the Adam man is the cerebellum. You won't get any of this in church because this is esoteric truth. Exoteric truth denies this and has been perpetuated for the last few thousand years by so-called Christian churches in order to deny and hide the true story of physical regeneration. In the past, people lived for thousands of years by preserving and conserving this oil and transmuting it so that it would reach the optic thalamus.

When the oil reaches the optic thalamus, new blood is generated in the body. Until this process occurs, we will have old toxic blood in our physical organisms and in order to regenerate and produce new blood, the oil must be raised to the optic thalamus for healing to occur. As I said before, millions of dormant brain cells are reactivated, and the heavens, the cerebrum, were awaiting the return of the prodigal son. We all have dormant brain cells in our brain because the oil has not been returned.

In the Bible, this is known as tithing and this is why the Bible says you must return one tenth to the Lord.

Remember, the Lord, the L-O-R-D refers to the gold, and this is how we turn lead into gold. Our spinal cord is like a thermometer, and just as the mercury rises with warmth, with enlightenment, consciousness and knowledge, we are able to raise the condition of the oil. As the oil climbs the spine and ascends, it raises its vibration. In fact, it gets crucified at the top of the spine where the pneumogastric nerve is crossed but this does not mean death.

Crucifixion means to multiply a thousandfold. You will realise that it not only results in physical regeneration, but also spiritual regeneration. In this way one is able to experience the higher mind and clairvoyance. Mediumship occurs down in the solar plexus. There are four brains in the human body: the cerebrum, otherwise known as the God brain, the cerebellum, which is the man brain, the medulla oblongata, which is responsible for the involuntary actions in the body, such as breathing and blood circulation, and the fourth brain is the solar plexus. The solar plexus is more related to the animal instinctive brain, which receives images from the ether or from the air, just as animals do. Animals react correspondingly without reason and logic, instinctively. This is why it is so important to raise the oil so that one can get out of the lower mind.

The lower mind, the solar plexus, is wrought with problems, since ascension is within and one ascends to heaven, the heaved up place, the dome of the cerebrum. Those two flaps, those hollowed out hemispheres of the cerebrum are otherwise known as the cherubim. In the Bible, God says to Moses, "You must build the Ark of the Covenant with two cherubim above the Ark, covering over. And inside the ark shall be placed the manna and the law of God, the two tablets." Well, I'm here to tell you that the optic thalamus is the ark of the covenant and the limbic system, the midbrain, the pons, the medulla oblongata and the pineal gland are the holy of holies. This is where one needs to return the good oil.

In the middle of the head, there is something known as the hippocampus, also known as the little horse. This is the white horse that Jesus rides upon. There is something known as Ammon's horn in the middle of the head. We have the claustrum. We have the cerebrum, which is the covering angels, the cherubim, which cover over, because the cerebrum covers over the cerebellum, the midbrain, the optic thalamus, the pineal gland and the pituitary gland, otherwise known as Joseph and Mary. You see, these two glands are responsible for sending the oil down the spinal cord. They are await the return of their son who is born in Bethlehem, the solar plexus, once a month, when the moon is in the sun sign under which you were born.

In the Hindu system this is called soma juice. When the oil descends into the third ventricle, the third heaven, it gets differentiated and the pineal gland produces the positive fluid, while the pituitary body produces the negative fluid. The positive fluid goes down the pingala red all the way down to the sacrum here. The pituitary body sends the negative fluid down the ida, and this is the sushumna in the middle.

Thus, you have the two Kundalini serpents, and the oil is differentiated here in the third ventricle, and it comes to the sacrum. This is where Scorpio is. You'll find this information in ten natural treatments you haven't heard of until now, such as William Wong. The sacrum forms the bottom pump for the cerebrospinal fluid respiration. The sphenoid and occipital bones at the floor of the brain form the top of the pump. When you breathe, these cranial bones teeter-totter against each other at their meeting point in the centre bottom of the skull and this action pumps brain fluid around the brain case and down the spinal canal.

Again, when you breathe, the sacrum rocks minutely front and back, pumping the fluid back up. This happens every month when the moon is transiting your sun sign.

Every 29 days the moon goes through each of the twelve signs and spends two and a half days in each sign. When the moon is in your sun sign she births a psychophysical germ in your solar plexus, which has twelve nerves. The sacrum is Virgo, Bethlehem, where Baby Jesus is born. Jesus was the child of Joseph and Mary, so Joseph is the pineal gland, and Mary is the pituitary gland.

If we look after this very tender seed, it eventually will ascend and it will activate each chakra as it returns back to head heaven. This oil is called a secretion. Notice the word sacred, and here is the sacrum. It's the sacred secret that the Apostle Paul was talking about in Colossians 1:26-27. The Jehovah's Witness Bible calls it a sacred secret that was not known to the ancients, and the secret is the Christ within me, not without.

There are 33 bones in the spinal column, and when you get to the last one and you cross the medulla oblongata here at the bottom of the head, there are twelve cranial nerves. The 33rd bone is where the Christ is crucified, at the vagus nerve. This is the nerve that goes through your body. It's a vagrant and it just wanders around through the body, feeding the heart, the liver, the spleen, the kidneys and all the vital organs, and then it returns all the fluid back to the cerebrum.

In the Book of Revelation, it mentions the Lamb of God 29 times. How are sheep related to salvation? And the holiest of books, every chapter. The Book of Revelation has 22 chapters because of the 22 paths of the Kabbalistic Tree.

We shall see what the Lamb of God has got to do with all of us. The Lamb of God is the two hemispheres of the cerebrum. The corpus callosum is the Red Sea where we go from the sinister brain, sinister is sin. Sinners are people who insist that their cleverness is above all knowing. They say, "Oh, my opinions, I'm going to repeat them. They're all wrong, and I'm going to keep them till I go to my grave. Oh, I'm going to be a Catholic till I die. I will die a Catholic, an ignoramus, a supporter of paedophilia." That's what this sinister brain does. We have to cross the corpus callosum to get into the Holy Land in the East, in the right, because right is right. Left is not right, it's sin.

The vagus nerve is also called the pneumogastric nerve because it feeds the stomach and the lungs. Once the oil crosses this nerve, it then enters into the third ventricle and touches the optic thalamus, the Lamb of God, Orion. Lamb is also lamp because it's the lamp that sees the eye, the simple eye. When you keep your eyes simple, your whole body will be illuminated because when the oil returns and gets crucified here, Joseph and Mary, the pineal gland and the pituitary gland, you become very, very happy. The oil then goes into the third ventricle, which is called the Cave of Brahma, where Brahma is dead for three days, or Jesus is lying in a tomb for three days, after which activation occurs.

The pineal gland is touched with this oil. The pineal gland already produces melatonin and dimethyltryptamine. It commences to produce something which is called the blood of the Christ. This is Christ turning water into wine. This is what is called the good wine in occult science . Finally, we have wine, not water in our blood. And this blood of the Christ cleans the blood, purifies the blood, administers the 12 salts that we need, and we can live virtually forever if we do this process. This is why hermits live to 300 or 400 years. I show evidence of people living 600 years, 300 years, or celebrating their 400th birthday in many of my presentations. You won't hear this in our conventional media, but it is a fact. And here we are dying at 60, 70 and 80 years.

"Oh, he died at 80. Had nice long life." Rubbish. That's a short life because that person squandered their oil. They used up all their good oil. Although you nurture the oil by returning the oil back.

We do so by not over drinking. When you see all these pubs around Amsterdam filled with young people with glasses of beer, that's killing the oil. Alcohol is poison. It's toxic. In moderation, it's okay. It can be medicinal, originally. A little wine can be good for the digestion, but not a party.

There's the tree that God planted in the Garden of Eden, and here is the fornix, right in the centre of the brain. Here are the anterior pillars of the fornix. These are the pillars of Hercules. This is where we need to bring the oil. There's the ram. It's easy to see that the cerebrum, Aries, is in the shape of the bulls. These are the horns of the ram and there are the two pillars, through which the oil has to be brought. These are the pillars of Hercules. This is Jesus returning back to heaven, resurrecting.

Once the oil passes into the third ventricle, it stays

dead in the tomb for three days. Then the stone is removed, an electrical impulse is sent through those two pillars and it goes through into the right side of the brain, known as the east or the right, and then it activates all the dormant brain cells. We have dormant brain cells in our cerebrum and that's why you see all these people sleeping.

Jesus says, "In the days of the end, people will be eating and drinking, buying and selling until the flood came and swept them all away." The flood is the flood of consciousness. It always is. There are two kinds of destruction in the scriptures, water and fire, The fire is Promethean fire, which comes and destroys all those who are sleeping. Hence, sleeping is very dangerous.

The Pillars of Hercules are in your head. God, generation, geometry, Gaia, grail, the Holy Grail. The Holy Grail is the third ventricle. In the Bible, 1st Kings 6:8, the door for the middle chamber, the pineal gland, was in the right side of the house, or the right hemisphere of the brain. And they went up winding stairs into the middle chamber and out of the middle, into the third.

The apostle Paul said, "I went to the third heaven." And Jacob laid his head on the Stone of Scone, that's the sacrum down here, and he saw a ladder going up to heaven with angels descending and ascending. Then he went up the ladder, saw God face-to-face and survived. Afterwards he said, "I've seen God face-to-face and I live and I call this place–"

"... pineal, pineal, the pineal place." That's the pineal gland and the third ventricle.

The twelve signs of the zodiac are in the head. Aries is here, Taurus is the eyes, Gemini the nostrils, Cancer, Leo, Virgo is in here, and Libra is the two olives here. Before Jesus was crucified, He was on the Mount of Olives.

There are two pyramids and there is the pons. Pons is bridge and it's the bridge to heaven, the head. We need the pons to get from cerebellum to the cerebrum. There are pyramids in Egypt because the pyramids are there at the delta. The delta is in your head and Egypt is exactly the same as the skies.

Many philosophers said that the soul was in the head, in the cerebrum. Plato held that the vital principle was in the brain and that the brain and spinal cord were coordinators of vital force, while Strato placed it in the forefront part of the brain between the eyebrows. Hippocrates placed the consciousness of the soul in the brain. Herophilus held that the calamus scriptorius was the chief seat of the soul. Herostratus believed that the soul was in the cerebellum or the little brain. Galen believed that the fourth ventricle of the brain was the home of the soul. Hippolytus held that the spirit advanced toward the pineal gland and the cerebellum. Saint Augustine believed it was the middle ventricle. The Arabian philosophers believed the brain was the seat of the soul. Dr. Hollander considers the reason why the ancient philosophers, from whom the Arabs adopted this localization and placed the faculties in certain cells, meaning cavities or ventricles, was probably to give more room for the gaseous substance to expand.

The third ventricle was the seat of understanding and the fourth was sacred to memory, which is the River Jordan in the head.

Other philosophers considered the two ventricles, the right and left lateral ventricles which communicate with one another and are continuous with the third ventricle. See that word, foramen? That means the hole of amen. The hole at the bottom of your cranium, where the spinal cord enters is called the hole of amen, foro di amen, and you have hundreds of foramens in your body. Amun is life, sun, the God of life. in Jesus' name, amen, and our bodies are full of amens, foramens.

Many great people, believed the soul was the centre of the brain, such as Roger Bacon and Ludovico Vives.

In summary,

1. The oil is differentiated in the pineal and pituitary gland before it is sent back down the spinal column. The pineal gland is the male electric honey. The pituitary gland is the magnetic feminine milk. Therefore, the oil is born in the medulla claustrum, and it makes the trip down to the sacrum.

2. In the cerebrum, there is the claustrum, the middle of the head. The claustrum secretes a brain fluid called the christus.

3. The christus oil leaves the cerebrum and pours down the spinal cord all the way down to the sacral plexus, which is next door to the sacrum. The oil comes to the lowest part of the sacral plexus.

4. Every month when the moon is in our sun sign, a germ or seed is planted in the solar plexus just above the sacral plexus, and the solar plexus is called Bethlehem, the birthplace of Christ. The seed oil needs to return from whence it came back to the mid-brain. As the oil ascends back up, it increases in vibration. The oil then arrives at the sacral plexus and awaits the germination of seed each month.

5. When it is time, we must work sacredly with the seed to increase it and make it raise in order for it to reach the medulla oblongata, the pond, the mid-brain. When it reaches the top of the mid-brain, it crosses over the vagus nerve, which is a nerve that descends from the pineal and pituitary gland. This nerve network is called the tree of life.

6. If we practice right action, this will cause the oil to be saved, not depleted, and rise and burst through the heart chakra to arrive back in the brain to cross the vagus nerve at the top of the spinal column.

7. When the raised oil returns at the 33rd vertebrae, the optic thalamus, an egg-shaped organ in the

middle of the head, awaits it. When the oil crosses this point, this is called the crucifixion, and at this point, the oil is magnified 1,000 fold. The oil touches the optic thalamus and the pineal gland.

8. In summary, this oil descends from the claustrum, from the cerebrum, is differentiated in the pineal and pituitary, and then descends down the spinal cord and awaits germination in the sacral plexus. It then ascends back up the spine to the optic thalamus, which causes enlightenment.

9. This turns on millions of dormant brain cells.

10. The oil must reach the optic thalamus in order to generate new blood in the body.

11. The parents, Mary and Joseph, create the oil which descends down the spinal column each month at the moon time. This action creates a seed in the sacrum, which is connected to the Kundalini energy. With right practices, the oil will rise, and will generate it back to the optic thalamus.

BIBLIOGRAPHY

The Hermetica Timothy Freak, and Peter Gandhi.

Tantric secrets- seven steps to the best sex of your life, shush- Cassandra, Lorius

Yoga of Time Travel, The : How the Mind Can Defeat Time Paperback – by Fred Alan Wolf PhD

Yoga Sutras of Patanjali – Patanjali.

Mountain Path. Dedicated to Bhagwan Shree Raman Maharshi

Trisulapura Mahatmyam The Glory and Grandeur of Tiruchuzhi

The Bhagvad Gita Eknath Easwaran

All about you by brother Manus

Guide to Giripradakshina published by Venkat S Ramanan

Existential Kink by Caroline Elliot, PhD.

Women Who Run With the Wolves, Clarissa Pinkola,

Twin Souls and Soulmates, St. Germaine, Clair Heart strong

HERE ARE THE LINKS TO JEN MCCARTY'S WEBSITE AND SOCIAL MEDIA

☐WEBSITE:https://www.jenmccarty144.com/

☐FACEBOOK:
htps://www.facebook.com/jen.mccarty23

Facebook group
https://www.facebook.com/groups/theeventishappening

☐INSTAGRAM:https://www.instagram.com/jenunionmccarty33/

☐TWITTER: https://twitter.com/jen_mccarty

TikTok
https://www.tiktok.com/@twinflamejenmccarty?lang=en

☐INSTAGRAM:https://www.instagram.com/jenunionmccarty33/

☐TWITTER: https://twitter.com/jen_mccarty

☐ YOUTUBE
https://www.youtube.com/channel/UC_8fJz5gAnhRqZ740QXlzmw

HERE ARE THE LINKS TO JEN MCCARTY'S BOOKS IN ORDER OF PUBLICATION

- Law of attraction little instruction book
  https://books2read.com/u/4j5g95

- TWIN FLAMES AND THE EVENT BOOK:
  mybook.to/Twinflamesbook

- TWIN FLAMES AND THE EVENT AUDIO:
  https://cosmicgypsy.sellfy.store/p/twin-flames-and-the-event-3iakku/

- TWIN FLAME AND THE EVENT WORKBOOK
  https://mybook.to/work-book-twin-flames

- NO MORE CRUMBS BOOK:
  mybook.to/nomorecrumbs

- NO MORE CRUMBS WORKBOOK
  rxe.me/DZPLLS

- NO MORE CRUMBS AUDIO :
  https://jenmccarty.co.uk/product/no-more-crumbs/

- DIVINE ACTOR I AM
  https://books2read.com/u/medPO9

- DIVINE ACTOR I AM AUDIO
  https://cosmicgypsy.sellfy.store/p/divine-actor-i-am-2iddvp/

- MANIFESTATION MASTERY

http://mybook.to/Manifestationmastery

- MANIFESTATION MASTERY AUDIO
  https://cosmicgypsy.sellfy.store/p/manifestation-mastery-audio/

- THE UNTENDED ALTER
  https://relinks.me/B0BRLX6HDBto

- THE UNTENDED ALTER AUDIO
  https://tinyurl.com/3yzfkufr

- THE JOURNEY TO UNION
  https://www.amazon.com/dp/B0C63P721G

- THE JOURNEY TO UNION AUDIO
  https://cosmicgypsy.sellfy.store/p/the-journey-to-union-audio/

- LITTLE BOOK OF NEVILLE GODDARD QUOTES https://tinyurl.com/w3y7db98

Made in United States
Cleveland, OH
18 May 2025